MAXIMIZING
BOARD
EFFECTIVENESS

GIRMA,

LEAS WEZU !

"One size does not fit all! Jim Galvin practically guides us through the maze of board structure options to help any size organization develop an effective board. The fluidity of his three base structures supplies great insight and direction to make every board function at its maximum contribution. Having been on many boards, this book has the ring of both truth and reality. Every board member and organizational leader should read this excellent work."

Jerry E. White, Ph.D., International President Emeritus and Chairman Emeritus, The Navigators

"If you're looking for clarity for your board, its role, how it should best function, and how to optimize its contribution to the success of your organization—this book is for you! Jim has written it in straightforward, practical, layman's language that demystifies the jargon, differentiates board types, and clarifies the realities you're looking for in improved board performance and impact. This book is more than a great read. It's a valuable reference tool. It can be your game-changer."

Bill Anderson, former President and CEO, Christian Booksellers Association

"Help boards stamp out dysfunctional governance. This phrase is one of the framing statements in the opening pages and perfectly characterizes the content of the book. Jim has done an excellent job of creating a textbook for helping boards and the organizations they serve, understand their roles, and have access to tools that help them operate with excellence there. A must-read!"

Greg Ligon, former Chief Innovation Officer, Leadership Network

"Jim Galvin has tremendous practical and everyday experience shepherding CEOs and boards in how they govern their organizations and ministries. His new book is the result of Jim's research and the application of years of wisdom gained through guiding those charged with leading organizations. Personally, as the leader of a historic Jewish ministry I found the book to be very helpful, eminently readable and filled with sensible and practical advice."

Mitch Glaser, Ph.D., President, Chosen People Ministries

"In this book, Jim Galvin has compiled a thorough set of principles and techniques to help any new board get started or an existing board to achieve a higher level of performance. He creatively infuses examples, stories, and exercises to actively engage any reader. A very effective guide for either non-profit or for-profit boards."

Paul Rigby, former Managing Director, JP Morgan Chase & Co.

"After years of experience, Galvin thoughtfully goes beyond the essentials to the complexities and varieties of actual governance. His book offers real help and understanding for board members who want to be diligent about making meaningful contributions to their board's effectiveness."

Dave Coleman, former Program Director, M.J. Murdoch Charitable Trust

"I have been on boards of large and small nonprofits and I generally hate books on governance. But Jim Galvin, with his years of experience advising boards, gives practical perspective so many boards need. This book is fresh, insightful, accessible, thorough, and refreshing."

Byron Spradlin, President, Artists in Christian Testimony International

"In my professional and volunteer work with church and community boards, I have often recommended Jim Galvin as a consultant and resource. And now I'm excited to recommend this book to any board that is interested in functioning more effectively and in adding more value to the organization they serve. The practical concepts, examples, and tools will be a blessing to any board as they evaluate and improve the way they govern."

Tim Schwan, former Vice President of Church and Community Engagement, Thrivent

"Jim Galvin's book drives home that effective boards must take time to 'know thyself' to have healthy relationships and structures. This book doesn't give pat answers but is full of excellent practical advice that stimulates one to consider how a board functions and how it could improve. I am certain that if any board engages Galvin's work and implements these principles and practices, the organization will be much more effective!"

Baruch Brian Kvasnica, President, Jerusalem Seminary

"Great leaders agree to serve on a board and then go 'stupid,' often neglecting best practices to avoid making waves. This book shows us how we can contribute, challenge, and evaluate all while being supportive of organizational leaders. An effective board is the pathway to exponential growth!"

Doug Franklin, CEO, LeaderTreks

"Three years ago we hired Jim Galvin to help us do strategic planning at our organization. When he said the core of any strategy or strategic plan should fit on one side of one sheet of paper, I was sold! Straightforward, practical, and to the point, this book is a must-read for all board members."

Brad Meuli, President/CEO, Denver Rescue Mission

"Jim Galvin has done it again. He has the gift of pulling together concepts, ideas, reflections, experiences, and meaningful and effective portraits to enable church leaders to better comprehend and take seriously the significance of effective and exciting board management in their congregations and other ministry settings. His clarifications and distinctions between managing Boards, governing Boards, and navigating boards is worth reading alone. I promise—you won't be Bored!"

Rich Bimler, Ed.D., CEO Emeritus, Wheat Ridge Ministries

"As a consultant and professor who teaches leaders how to do governance, I am familiar with what is available on the market for boards. This new book stands out among the rest because it is the best one for explaining what kind of board organizations need. Wondrously, this book is filled with business sense that makes great sense. If enough of us will sit down and read it, it just might make it common for boards to get past their notorious confusion and dysfunction and instead learn how to add value."

Sarah Sumner, Ph.D., MBA, President, Right On Mission

"Jim Galvin has become one of my absolute gurus when it comes to board governance. His understanding and practical application of what it takes to make governance work, especially in faith-based institutions, is far and above the best that is currently available. This book is a testament to his deep belief (and mine) that good governance supports and facilities great ministry."

Donald Christian, D.M., President and CEO, Concordia University Texas

"This book is a must-read for those that desire to turn board success from a dream to reality. This practical and insightful book will help leaders make immediate and meaningful impact on board results. Get your highlighter ready to work hard!"

Dave Schunk, President and CEO, Volunteers of America Colorado

"This book is Jim Galvin's gift to the world of nonprofit governance. Every page is filled with practical insights to equip organizational leaders as they make decisions, establish policy, and set direction. Use this book as a continuous improvement tool for your board; it will help you assess your board's performance, educate new board members, and increase board effectiveness."

David Alexander, Ph.D., former President, Northwest Nazarene University

"Once again, Dr. Galvin does deep thinking to solve problems for faith-based and not-for-profit communities. Exploring beyond the known, he offers innovative thinking to improve board functions and, especially, organizational excellence."

Norb Oesch, D.Min., former Executive Leader, Pastoral Leadership Initiative

In straight-forward, clear language, Jim Galvin provides an incisive analysis of board effectiveness. While acknowledging that managing boards and governing boards each have their place in the history of not-for-profit organizations, Dr. Galvin makes a strong case for the importance of navigating boards which help reinvent and repurpose organizations, especially in uncertain and turbulent times. This is a thoughtful and helpful book for those who lead organizations in our uncertain and turbulent times."

Kurt Krueger, Ph.D., President Emeritus, Concordia University Irvine

"Are you in search of an exceptional resource for new board members, to remedy board governance confusion, or to transition a board for optimal effectiveness? Look no further! This instructional book is a topnotch handbook for board members to understand their responsibilities and to improve mechanics in all areas."

Susan Hewitt, Ed.D., Board member

"If you are looking for a definitive guide for working with your board, this is a must read from an author who has advised hundreds of non-profit organizations for over 20 years. I have personally benefited from Jim's knowledge and expertise and can say he is right on target with his assessment of more effective and less effective boards."

Ken Ellwein, former Executive Director, Orange Lutheran High School

"Jim has a thorough understanding regarding about not-for-profit organizations and how they should be properly governed by board of directors. During our strategic planning retreat, Jim was instrumental in helping our organization find the appropriate direction to ensure our success well into the future. For anyone who needs to learn about the appropriate roles of a board, Jim has the answers."

Sarah Ponitz, J.D., Executive Director, PADS of Elgin

"I have chaired, participated on and been responsive to boards in the for-profit, non-profit, religious, secular and public realms. Jim Galvin is a theoretical and experiential treasure trove of organizational management, governance and navigation knowledge and application, especially at the pivot point where boards meet the organizational leader. Even if you think you are pretty good at this process, this book will open unique and enlightened perspectives for organizational effectiveness and fulfillment."

John D. Eckrich, M.D., Physician and Founder, Grace Place Wellness Ministries

MAXIMIZING BOARD EFFECTIVENESS

A Practical Guide for Adaptive Governance

JAMES C. GALVIN

TENTH
POWER

TENTHPOWERPUBLISHING

www.tenthpowerpublishing.com

Design by Inkwell Creative

Softcover ISBN 978-1-938840-33-3
e-book ISBN 978-1-938840-34-0

10 9 8 7 6 5 4 3 2 1

CONTENTS

FOREWORD

My calendar just turned to May 2020. The planet is in crisis because of the corona virus. We are watching many elements of what life was, now turn into anxious uncertainty about the future. Many are wondering if their organization will survive and remain sustainable?

If you are a nonprofit leader, this book has dozens of good answers. Board members figuring out how to govern during this pandemic or in a future crisis will find help. Exhausted chief executives will see their role more clearly. Most are coming around to the conclusion that we will never return to what was normal. No, almost everything we've done is going to change–if our organizations can just survive.

Jim Galvin is one of those governance consultants who could honestly say, "I've seen it all." Until now. Well before COVID-19, Jim began sharing what makes some boards effective and others mostly dysfunctional. This book is full of Jim's clear, direct, totally understandable, plain talk counsel. I commend you for getting started on this book. For you, the sooner you spend a couple of hours marking up the text that resonates with you, the easier the path forward.

The common message of many during this virus is, "We are in this together." And that should apply to any of the 1.5 million-plus incorporated nonprofits and 350,000 churches in the US. Every one of them must have a board. All but the smallest have a designated chief organizational leader. Together, the board and organizational leader are the main people who will determine whether their missions survive or collapse. All of them should read this book and come to a consensus about what is right for them. There is simply no time to waste.

I am intrigued by Jim's confident statement that there are only three types of boards. All boards are derivatives of one of these types. I happen to be a governance consultant, too. The book has me thinking of clients with good governing boards that need to be challenged now to become navigating boards. Jim clearly describes the pros, cons, whys, and hows of each. Some who read the differences will decide they need a task force of outside people who can help in areas the current board is ill-equipped to do well. Many choices. But decide you must.

Whichever of the three types of boards you are, the next year and more is becoming the most challenging yet for many nonprofits. If you have depended on gathering people in groups to work, learn, or serve, what's next in this "social distancing" environment? Will investments in technology be wise? Can you absorb a significant decrease in giving? If your board members are themselves consumed with how they, their families, their businesses, or their churches will survive, how can that board design the organization's roadmap for an uncertain future? Some are already exploring a merger. Others are asking how to dissolve their organization with dignity. This common colloquialism now seems very real: "Only God knows." But every board must step up, be more effective than ever, and make the difficult decisions in a timely manner. No going back.

Robert C. Andringa, Ph.D., former CEO, Education Commission of the States
Scottsdale, Arizona
May 2, 2020

INTRODUCTION

This book is for those who chair a board, those who serve on a board, as well as those who report to a board. It was written to help boards stamp out dysfunctional governance.

Adaptive governance refers to boards that can shift their governing approach or mode when needed. Sometimes a board needs to lean in and get more involved in organizational decision making. Sometimes a board needs to step back and focus on policy. Sometimes a board needs to pay more attention to how the relevant environment is changing. If it is difficult for an organization to change, it is twice as hard for its board. Board members rarely reflect on their governing style or type. Just like our organizations need adaptive leadership today, they also benefit from adaptive governance.

There are a wide variety of words used to describe boards and governance. Let's keep the terminology simple.

- The group of people who oversee the organization are variously called the board of directors, board of trustees, council, or elder board. This book will use the term *board*.
- The person who leads the board is called the chairman, chairwoman, chair, president, or CGO (chief governance officer). This book will refer to this person as the *board chair*.
- The people who serve on the board are variously called, trustees, directors, representatives, or at-large members. This book will call them *board members*.
- The individual selected by the board to lead the organization is alternatively titled director, executive director, executive leader, president, senior pastor, principal, manager, or CEO (chief executive officer). This book will refer to this individual as the *organizational leader*.

I want to thank Peter O'Donnell, a colleague who walked alongside me as I worked on this manuscript from the first rough outline to the final draft. He did not laugh when I postulated that there are three types of boards. This book asserts that the purpose of a board is to ensure sustainable mission fulfillment. I borrowed this concept from his writing. He pressed me to develop a fuller definition of *navigating boards* and provided constructive feedback on every chapter.

CHAPTER 1

WHY BOARDS UNDERPERFORM

In theory, governance is straightforward. In real life, not so much. Most boards fail to reach their potential. Many boards even manage to make things worse for the organization they are supposed to oversee. Boards are supposed to make a significant contribution to their organizations, not waste time, money, and other resources. Why are so many boards ineffective? Why are so many boards dysfunctional?

Let me lead you through a thought experiment. Suppose you joined with five or six friends, invested a significant chunk of your savings, and secured a bank loan to build a minimart. Think: BP, Circle K, 7-Eleven, Love's, Pilot Flying J, ExtraMile, QuickChek, QuickTrip, Kwik Fill, Kwik Stop. You get the idea.

These are the combination gas station and convenience stores located at busy intersections where you can refill your gas tank, buy a coffee or soft drink, and common food items with one stop. (Note:

In real life, you should probably avoid buying your food and your fuel from the same store.)

Your investment group was able to secure a great location, plus get the building and infrastructure completed on time. Next, you need to order the fuel, stock the merchandise, and hire people to staff it. But you do not want to work in the minimart. Nobody in the group even wants to manage it. As a group, you want to *own* it and watch it throw off cash. So, you must hire a manager to do this work for you.

After a thorough recruiting process and a dozen interviews, you find a young woman who is a recent graduate from the state university. She was a business major and appears to have excellent people skills. She seems perfect to everyone and is eager to meet the challenge of opening a new store. So, you hire her to be the manager.

As the manager, you ask her to hire the rest of the team to run the minimart. You specify hiring only part-time workers to avoid paying benefits. You also ask her to schedule all the fuel deliveries, order all the inventory for the store, coordinate with the accountant, and keep the place looking nice. In other words, she is in charge.

For clear communication and accountability, you ask her to meet with you as a group once a month in a regular board meeting. In the meeting, you ask her to go over the financial statements with you, inform you on any problems she has encountered, any significant staff issues, or anything else she might want help with. Her job is to make a profit for the owners. In return, you agree to give her free reign to make daily decisions and run the business for you.

Reflection:

- Are you comfortable with this arrangement for overseeing the manager?
- Do you feel a need for more control?

- Will you ask for more detailed information about the business in your monthly owner meetings?
- Do you want her to check with you before making "big" decisions?

Opening day arrives. The Chamber of Commerce conducts the ribbon cutting ceremony. You are now a business owner. It feels exciting. You have your first monthly meeting and the minimart is profitable after its first month of operation. The manager is enthusiastic and easy to work with.

After six months, the minimart continues to be consistently profitable. Each month, the manager comes in with the financial reports and informs the board of any significant problems she had and how she solved them. Board meetings tend to last an hour or so each month. The manager continues to demonstrate excellent people skills with the staff and the board. Owning a business is easy!

As a group, you try to stay out of the mundane details of running the minimart. But you do purchase your gas there. After all, you are not going to buy your gas from a competitor. You might also stop in to buy a "healthy" snack from time to time. So, you cannot help but notice the store is not looking brand new anymore. The tile often has a gray haze from wet shoes on rainy days. The products on the shelves appear disorganized. The counter is crowded with odds and ends. As a group, the owners begin talking to each other about their concerns. After all, they want the business to throw off as much cash as possible.

Reflection:

- How should you address your concerns?
- Should you remain silent because the business is making a tidy profit?

- Should each board member speak to the manager and comment every time they visit the minimart?
- Should you bring up these concerns at the next board meeting?
- What action would you want the board to take?

At the next meeting, the manager cheerfully brings another positive financial report. She explains that two employees have given notice, but she has already hired replacements. As a group, you have decided to bring your concerns to her during the board meeting. You want to share these concerns in as gentle of a way as possible. You share the concern about the dirty floor, and she explains that the floor is mopped after closing every day. The board instructs her to have an employee mop more often during inclement weather. You bring up the messiness of product on the shelves and ask her to pay more attention to how the inside of the store looks to customers. She agrees to have employees spend more time organizing the shelves. Then you explain how terrible the counter looks. You tell her to clear all the junk off so that people can more easily pay their bill. She agrees but looks a bit dismayed. You thank her for her good work and assure her of your confidence in her as the manager.

After the meeting, you all agree that as a board you shared these requests as politely and gently as possible. You all agree that other than these few exceptions, the manager is doing a great job.

Next month, the manager explains that profit is down a bit but that she has fully implemented the changes requested by the owners. She is as upbeat as normal. The following month, she brings a financial report showing the profit has gone down to zero. The board sits in stunned silence for a while. Then one of the board members cannot hold back. "What's going on? How could profit drop to zero? Do you have an attitude problem?"

The manager takes a deep breath and patiently explains, "You told me to take all the impulse items off the counter. Where do you think your profit comes from? It is not from selling gas. I had to add an hour to the shift of some employees to straighten the shelves during the day. They all get straightened at night anyway. Messy shelves are a good thing. They are an indicator of customer traffic. Oh, and we have had three elderly people slip on the floor during the past few weeks after mopping. I think we should go back to mopping only after closing to avoid personal injury lawsuits."

Reflection:

- Was the board right to be concerned about the sloppy appearance of the business?
- Was the board right in asking the manager to make certain small changes?
- Were any boundaries overstepped?
- Should the board have kept their collective mouth shut?

Unintentionally, the owners made things worse. They thought they were being helpful, even smart, but they reduced the value of their business. They unintentionally made matters worse. Nonprofit boards often do the same. They ask detailed questions about the budget, get involved in operations, and give counterproductive advice to the organizational leader.

Becoming an effective board is not as easy as it sounds. Effective boards make a significant contribution but stay out of the weeds.

ALL BOARDS NEED TO MAKE A CONTRIBUTION

Most people would agree that all boards of nonprofits should make a net contribution to the organization. But merely holding a board meeting only uses up resources. Hearing reports does not contribute value. Asking questions about the budget does not contribute value. Approving requests by the organizational leader does not contribute value. Let me explain using widgets.

Consider the processes of a manufacturing line making widgets. One worker brings in sheets of metal to the first station. The sheets are cut into 8" by 8" squares. The next station drills four holes near the corners. Then another part is bolted onto those squares. Next it is spray painted and put under heat lamps. When dry, it is boxed for shipment. A quality inspector stands at the end of the line. He opens a box, looks at the widget, make sure it functions properly. Then he puts a small sticker on it that says it is approved and puts it back in the box.

According to W. Edwards Deming and the lean manufacturing community, the quality inspector at the end of a manufacturing line adds no value to the product or the company. It is a pure expense, even an unnecessary one. In fact, if the inspector drops a widget and damages it, he is eroding value to the company. To add value, the quality inspections must be built into the process and occur during manufacturing.

When the first worker brings in the sheets of metal, he should assure it is from the right stock. After the sheet is cut into a square, that worker should check that the size of all pieces is exactly 8" by 8". After the holes are drilled, the piece should be placed over a template with four dowel rods to ensure correct spacing. After painting, the person unloading the parts should check for flaws in the finish.

Quality needs to be built into the system at every step.

Similarly, when boards view budget reports from the previous month or quarter, they are like the quality inspector at the end of the line. They cannot add any value to the organization by hearing activity reports and approving requests made by the organizational leader.

If I am working with a board with experienced executives, I sometimes share this illustration at the beginning of the day and ask, "So, how does the board add value to this organization?" They usually struggle to answer.

Many boards unintentionally make things worse for the organizational leader and organization at times. If they feel unsure about making a major decision and ask for more information or more time to discuss what to do, it ties the hands of the leader. The organization cannot move forward until the next board meeting. If the board wants to be involved with interviewing candidates for all significant positions, they complicate the hiring process without increasing the quality of the candidate pool. If they reject all the candidates brought forward, they are unintentionally doubling the cost of the entire hiring process.

Dysfunctional boards do not add value. They erode value. They fail to make a net contribution. They use up valuable time of the director, create conflict, slow down decision making, block urgent strategic moves, give unwelcome advice, make poor decisions, distract leaders from their work, and otherwise cause problems. Obviously, board members who do not speak up during a board meeting do not make a contribution. They are taking up space and using up oxygen.

COUNTING THE COST

Boards are put in place by law to oversee nonprofit organizations and make sure they comply with all governmental regulations. Ideally, they should be contributing to the nonprofit rather than wasting time, money, and other resources. However, most boards cannot describe precisely how they contribute value.

As an exercise, calculate how much it costs for your organization to plan, prepare, and hold all your board meetings over the course of a year. If you are a larger organization and reimburse for travel, include that. If you pay for lodging and meals, include that. Then calculate the time it takes your director and staff to prepare for the meetings, write all the reports, compile handouts, and sit in the meetings. Add up their hours worked and multiply by their hourly wage.

Next, ask what benefits the board brings to offset those expenses. It will take a significant contribution to get up to the breakeven point. (Warning: This can be a sobering exercise.)

Individual board members can bring boardroom capital. This can include such things as significant financial contributions, strategic thinking, network connections, knowledge of the industry or relevant environment, experience in governance, spiritual discernment, and wisdom.

If a board is eroding value, the organization would be better off if they met as seldom as permissible by law. If the board members are not regular donors, they are bringing a net negative stewardship to the organization. But legal requirements or organizational bylaws often specify that a board is appointed to oversee the work of the nonprofit organization. So, many boards meet and are unsure how to govern. This is not easy because there is a lot of contradictory advice and confusion surrounding governance.

CHAPTER 2

GOVERNANCE CONFUSION

Ask for advice from a couple friends about your golf swing and you are highly likely to receive conflicting tips. Similarly, ask experienced board members about governance practices and you are highly likely to receive contradictory guidance. Professional governance consultants might give you different advice. Even authors of books on governance give conflicting instruction. It's even worse than golf.

Where do you land regarding some of this conflicting advice? Where does your board land? Place an X in the scale below.

ON THE ONE HAND...		ON THE OTHER HAND...
The organizational leader should be a full member of the board with a formal vote.		The organizational leader should report to the board and not have a formal vote.

You should have term limits to rid the board of deadwood and members who need a break.		Let turnover happen naturally. Term limits lead to an automatic brain drain.
You don't need any more than five or six committed board members. How many people does it take to oversee the organization?		You should have a larger board because it gives you access to so much more talent and potential donors.
Don't bother moving to policy-based governance. You want an active and engaged board, not a bunch of people wordsmithing policies.		Most boards should transition to policy-based governance. This directly addresses some of the frustrations the organization is facing.
Include key staff people as a regular part of your board meetings.		Don't include any staff people as a regular part of your board meetings.
Keep board committees to a bare minimum. Use ad hoc committees on a temporary basis if needed.		A good board will have several standing committees such as finance and governance.
Recruit people such as corporate managers, small business owners, and professionals to bring the talent you need to the board.		Recruit people who want to oversee the organization and can refrain from getting involved in operational matters.

The board should delegate authority and avoid telling the organizational leader how to manage the organization.		Board members have a wealth of experience and should offer advice to the organizational leader for improving the organization.
Periodically, the board should review and revise the mission statement and core values document of the organization.		The mission statement and core values document are management tools that should be revised and updated by the staff.
A good board will strive to achieve consensus on every important decision even if it takes more time.		Consensus is good but not practical. After enough discussion, the board should vote.
Every board needs a capable treasurer to oversee the finances of the organization.		If your state or province does not require a treasurer, then do not appoint one.
If you have an under-performing board, ask for resignations and find more capable people.		If you have an under-performing board, work with who you have and ask for renewed commitment from all.
After a new board is in place, the board should select its own chair from the members of the board.		The chair of the board is an officer and should be elected separately from the board members-at-large.

The board chair is the leader of the board and should lead like he or she would lead any other team.	☐☐☐☐☐☐	The board chair is the leader of the board and should focus on making sure all members are heard.
A board should recruit people to represent the differing constituencies that are a part of the organization.	☐☐☐☐☐☐	A board should recruit people capable of representing the whole of the organization and not any single constituency.
Invite people with major donor potential to serve on your board and get them involved with fundraising.	☐☐☐☐☐☐	Rather than inviting major donors to serve on your board, create a separate affinity group for them.
Every board should use the procedures in *Robert's Rules of Order* for board discussions.	☐☐☐☐☐☐	Please, no. Strive for natural conversation using good principles of dialogue instead.

CONFUSION LEADS TO INEFFECTIVENESS

All the contradictory advice to board members produces confusion about how to govern on any board. Governance confusion is a leading cause of board ineffectiveness. Board members need absolute clarity about the mission of their organization, the purpose of the board, how the board should function, and their role as board member. Clarity is crucial because governance confusion can produce unwanted consequences such as these.

Awkward structure: Board members often feel uncertain about whether their board should be larger or smaller. They add standing committees that make meetings unnecessarily complex and waste the time of busy members. With some boards meeting once a month and others only three times a year, they wonder how often to meet. They feel uncertain about whether to keep or extend term limits.

Recruitment ambiguity: Board members wonder whether they should recruit aggressive leaders or team players or both. They wonder whether to ask people who represent their key donor groups or beneficiaries or both. They struggle over whether to fill the board with people who have major donor potential. This confusion also leads to weak orientation experiences.

Misaligned leadership: Board chairs can feel uncertain about their role in the meetings. It can lead to a board chair who is paralyzed or overbearing. Governance confusion opens the door to the organizational leader trying to run the board as well as the organization.

Disagreement over process: Board members can get confused about how to get their work done. They wonder whether it is better to vote or strive for consensus. Board chairs don't know when to call an end to a long meeting. Confusion can lead to overly detailed reporting on operations and programming. Some feel uncertain about when and how to appoint a temporary committee.

Disengaged members: Confusion about board member roles and responsibilities can lead to increasing board member disengagement. Without clear expectations, board members arrive unprepared for the meeting. Some don't show up and don't let anyone know ahead of time.

Unclear boundaries: Governance confusion leaves board members uncertain about when and how to intervene in operations. Some board members desire to take more action and end up dragging the entire board into the weeds. It leads to lack of clarity of who makes what decisions: Board, staff, or both together.

Vague strategy: Confusion also leads to weak organizational strategy. Board members can feel uncertain about whether they develop the strategy or simply approve it. They don't know if commenting on long-range strategy is stepping over the line. Some might wonder if their small nonprofit even needs a long-range strategy.

Unacceptable behavior: If a board has any level of governance confusion and you add unhealthy group dynamics, governance quickly becomes even more confusing. If a board member, officially elected by the organizational constituency, regularly yells and pounds the table during board meetings, what should be done? If a governing board devolves into two opposing groups, how can it be united? Interpersonal conflict and board members with unacceptable behavior can derail the agenda of any meeting. Boards have a hard time making a positive difference if they can't get along.

This widespread confusion surrounding governance can grow into a breeding ground for frustration. How can a board sort through this governance confusion? Wait, it gets even more complicated.

VARIETIES OF BOARDS

Different organizations need different types of boards. Just consider the amazing array of nonprofit organizations: Universities, social service agencies, tutoring ministries, homeless shelters, congregations, denominations, animal rescue groups, sports for children, museums, foundation boards, homeowner associations, and hospitals.

Hospitals, especially, are large and complex organizations. It is literally a life and death enterprise. All hospitals have a board, yet none of the board members know how to manage a hospital, supervise physicians, or control a budget as enormous as what is set before them.

In fact, for most of them their only real qualification is that they have been to the doctor. How is the board going to add value to the hospital?

To add to the complexity, a nonprofit organization may have several boards that govern different areas. For example, a local congregation may have a mission board, youth board, fellowship board, finance board, children's ministry board, facilities board, worship board, education board, and an investment committee. A large, national nonprofit may have regional boards that make decisions and determine policy in their territory. A nonprofit with a highly federated structure may have hundreds of local boards or committees that are largely autonomous. A university may have a faculty group that shares governance with the governing board.

MOVING FROM CONFUSION TO CLARITY

Therefore, every board needs to reduce the confusion surrounding governance so they can figure out how to make a significant contribution to their nonprofit organization. Given the opportunity, most boards would want to achieve clarity on their purpose, board member roles, and how to make a significant contribution to their organization. Not always, but most of the time, they would want to reduce dysfunctional behavior in the board meetings and stop wasting the valuable time of the other board members. They would want to promote healthy change for the sustainability of their nonprofit. But board chairs and board members keep getting conflicting advice.

What if most of the conflicting advice was right, given different circumstances? What if different organizations need different kinds of boards? What if there were different types of boards that could be clearly differentiated?

What if there were only three types of boards?

THREE TYPES OF BOARDS

In addition to the various kinds of nonprofit organizations, there are many different flavors of boards. For example, some terms used by nonprofit organizations include:

- Board of directors
- Trustee board
- Operational board
- Policy board
- Board of reference
- Patron board
- Advisory board
- Fundraising board
- Management board
- Council of advisors
- President's council
- Executive board

- Leadership roundtable
- Governing board
- Futures council
- Vision board
- Ambassadors council
- Elder board
- Cabinet
- Board of observers
- Blue ribbon task force

Though many use the term "board," some of these do not have authority over the organization. They are auxiliary groups formed for a specific purpose such as fundraising or obtaining specific advice. But a fundraising board or advisory board typically has no legal authority over an organization. They are simply called "boards" by the organization to lend credibility or prestige. A more accurate term would be committee, council, roundtable, or task force.

BOARDS WITH AND WITHOUT AUTHORITY

When registering with the government, most states or provinces require that a board of directors be established. The board is placed in authority over the organization and its staff as a fiduciary. A fiduciary is legally bound to make decisions that are in the best interest of another. For nonprofit board members, the fiduciary duties have three aspects: duty of care, duty of loyalty, and duty of obedience.

Duty of Care: This means board members are exercising care in their position. They prepare adequately, actively participate in meetings, ask questions, and stay informed about governance. The legal expectation is that they are making decisions for the organization at the same level of care as a prudent person. In other words, they are not careless or disengaged.

Duty of Loyalty: This means board members have an undivided loyalty to the organization. They readily reveal any real, potential, or perceived conflicts of interest. They make decisions in the best interest of the organization, not for themselves or others. In other words, they avoid self-dealing and corruption.

Duty of Obedience: This means board members are ensuring that the organization is obeying all applicable laws. They also follow their own governing policies, stick to the ultimate purpose of the organization, and make sure assets are not diverted to noncharitable uses. In other words, they are not doing anything illegal or unethical.

So, a board with authority over a nonprofit is a legal requirement. The constitution, bylaws, or statutes of the organization clearly describe how board members are selected, the length of their terms, and the expectations of service.

Boards without authority may provide a useful function, but they do not count as true boards. They are serving some other purpose besides overseeing the organization. A true board represents the moral owners of the organization and has authority over it. They are legally able to hire and fire the organizational leader, approve or disapprove the budget, buy or sell property, change the mission of the organization, or shut it down.

If we strip away all the pseudo boards or board-like groups, and we focus on boards with legal authority over the organization, then we are left with a limited number of types of boards. Three, to be exact.

Systems theory can help us think more clearly about these three types and how boards can make a net contribution to their organization.

THE BLACK BOX

General systems theory was developed by the biologist Ludwig von Bertalanffy in the mid-twentieth century and captured in his book published in 1968. Systems theory is not complicated but attempts to show how everything is interrelated and interdependent. Any phenomenon can be described from a systems viewpoint. This includes nonprofit organizations and their boards.

A basic system has five aspects: input, process, output, feedback, and the environment. Inputs include everything coming into the system such as people, data, and things. Process is described as how the system acts on the inputs and what it does. Outputs describe what is coming out of the system as benefits or waste. Feedback is the information about the outputs that is fed back into the system as new information. Feedback allows the system to self-correct.

The environment includes all the outside forces acting on the system. The relevant environment is the space inside the dotted line. But forces outside the dotted line, which the system does not easily recognize, can intervene and impact the system. A relatively closed system will describe a limited relevant environment. A relatively open system will pay attention to other forces in the wider environment. The outputs of one system become the inputs of another system. The inputs of a system come from the outputs of other systems. Systems impact other systems and are connected in nonobvious ways.

Anything can be viewed from a systems perspective. For example, let's consider a widget factory. The input includes the employees, raw materials, customer orders, and other information. The process includes all the activities happening inside the widget factory such as manufacturing, supervision, and bookkeeping. The output includes the products, services, and benefits the company provides to others. Feedback includes quality assurance data, customer satisfaction ratings, and suggestions for improvement. The environment includes everything that is happening in the widget market and general economy that impacts the company.

We can adapt this general systems theory to a nonprofit context. Input becomes the resources coming into the organization, including staff, volunteers, charitable gifts, clients, and relevant information. The process becomes all the activities that happen inside the organization, both to serve clients and maintain the organization. The outputs can be interpreted as the results the organization is realizing. This includes immediate outcomes, intermediate outcomes, and ultimate outcomes. Feedback involves any information about process improvement or relative success in achieving organizational outcomes. It can be gathered by regular monitoring or by direct observation. The environment includes any outside forces acting on the organization.

For example, let's consider a tutoring ministry at a public grade school in an under-served neighborhood. Input includes students, volunteer tutors, curriculum materials, teaching methods, and funding to make it all happen. Activities include all that happens after school when students engage in tutoring, games, snacks, and study time. The results include student performance in class and positive attitude toward learning. Feedback includes attendance rates, measures of academic progress, graduation rates, and other useful data. The environment includes level of parent support, legal requirements, and the local political situation.

The board is a part of the nonprofit organization, but above the operational level. A board with authority is above the organization but still connected.

The activities happening inside the organization are like a black box to the board. They see the resources going in and the results

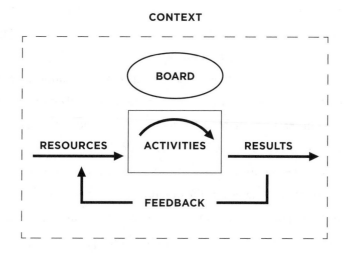

coming out, but they do not have detailed information about all the activities happening daily.

From a systems perspective, any board only has three options for how to deal with what is happening in the black box of operations. They can open the box and make decisions, they can oversee the box and set policies, or they can pick up the box and move it.

If a board wants to open the lid, look inside, and make decisions about activities or operations happening inside the box, then it is a managing board. If a board wants to keep the lid shut, delegate management, and set policy for what actions the organizational leader and staff may not take, then it is a governing board. If a board wants to change the mission of the organization, its clients, its services, or its geography, then it is a navigating board acting on the box directly and shaping it in a significant way.

How does the focus of these three differ? Managing boards focus on making decisions and improving procedures. Governing boards focus on organizational results and board policies. Navigating boards focus on making major shifts in the organization to exploit new opportunities or ensure a sustainable future.

Governing boards are not superior to managing boards or navigating boards. Each can be an appropriate response to what the organization needs at a certain point in time. Each can also be the wrong response to what an organization may need.

Managing boards open the black box and get involved in operational decision making. They are helping the organizational leader to manage the organization. Governing boards are above the box overseeing all that is happening. They stay out of the box and delegate the ongoing operations to the organizational leader. They focus on resources going in and results coming out. They ask if resources are adequate for sustainability and if the results justify the resources going in. Navigating boards keep an eye on the environment and determine whether major changes in the organization or its mission are needed.

For example, suppose a small ministry to homeless men has run a shelter in a part of a city that is slated for rapid development of high-rise offices and apartments. The homeless population they serve has shifted away from their current location. The city mayor has asked them to leave and if they don't, they will likely be forced out. But they own their building outright and this property has become extremely valuable. If they sold, they would be able to build a more modern facility and still have a net gain. This represents a prime opportunity for the ministry.

A managing board would get actively involved in deciding where and how to relocate. They would figure out the assessed value of their current property, estimate the long-range costs of maintaining their current building, and research several available parcels where they could build a new facility. The board would make these decisions as a group together with the organizational leader.

A governing board would note the need to relocate and think deeply about alternative ways to move forward. They would revisit their ends policies and ask the organizational leader to research all alternatives and come back with a proposal for relocating and renovating an existing property or building a new facility. They might set criteria for the proposed solution, such as access to public transportation or distance from grade schools. Alternatively, they might form a committee to do this work with the organizational leader serving on the committee. Later, the board would approve the proposal that best meets their criteria and helps achieve the desired outcomes of the ministry.

A navigating board would note the need to relocate and use this as a trigger to examine what else is changing in their relevant environment. They would look at other organizations ministering to homeless people and see where they might best fit in. They might discover the face of homelessness is changing and the need for men's shelters is adequately served, but the emerging need in their city is shelter for women and children. This kind of board might change their ends policies and their target audience, approach a struggling hotel that is not for sale, purchase it, renovate it, and revamp all their programs to serve women and children.

As another example, consider a once-vibrant youth ministry now struggling to survive. They have a difficult time attracting high school students to their outdated programs. They are seeing almost no teenagers coming to faith. What used to work so well in the 1970s does not work as well today. They have lost the ability to attract talented staff and volunteers, their donors are aging out, and now they are only a tenth of the size they were forty years ago. Part of the problem is that youth are busier than ever. They spend their time with cell phones, competitive sports, and video games. The youth ministry can't compete with technology and they don't know how to join it. They are also finding that the increasingly secularization of society is making youth more resistant to the gospel. How should the board respond?

A managing board would dig into the details, explore how to recruit more volunteers, secure new donors, hold more fundraisers, and improve the branding of the youth ministry. They might research new youth ministry methods. Their goal would be to work together with the organizational leader to get the ministry performing well again.

A governing board would dig into the details, refine their ends policies, and task the organizational leader with getting better results. They would give the organizational leader wide latitude to innovate and accomplish what needs to happen. Their goal would be to clarify expectations, support the organizational leader, and monitor implementation.

A navigating board would dig into the details of their context, look at the broader picture, observe how youth ministry is changing and how youth are changing. They might learn that the challenges they faced in high school are now faced by children in middle school. They might make a major shift to abandon high school ministry and launch a new focus on middle school students, or shift their whole approach to meeting the needs of students facing specific life challenges, such as preparing for college entrance exams, learning basic life skills, or dealing with substance abuse such as drinking or vaping. Their approach would be to start with a blank slate and consider all reasonable options.

THREE TYPES OF BOARDS

So, there are three types of boards, depending on how they deal with the black box. Any other board with authority is a derivative of one of these three types.

Each type of board requires a different focus, tools, and board member skills. Each way of functioning can be executed either more effectively or less effectively.

Different contributions: Managing boards want to improve operations and efficiency. Governing boards want to improve effectiveness and overall productivity. Navigating boards want to spot new opportunities, overhaul the existing system, or innovate to adapt to what is changing around them.

Different interventions: Managing boards intervene in operations all the time. This is how they get things done. Governing boards want to stay out of operations but will intervene in a crisis or failure of management to get things back to normal. Navigating boards intervene to make major changes and create a new normal.

Different skills: Managing boards need people with professional skills such as finance, HR, and legal. They need experienced managers, whether middle managers in large corporations or small business owners. Governing boards need people staying above the fray, staying out of operations, and focused on results. These are people who want

	MANAGING	GOVERNING	NAVIGATING
	EXECUTIVE MANAGEMENT	POLICY-BASED GOVERNANCE	TRANSFORMATIVE GOVERNANCE
MORE EFFECTIVE	Leadership team C-Suite skills Disciplined conversation High-level decision making Tactical planning Skillful delegation	Disciplined board members Proactive Results-oriented ends policies Clear limitations policies Strive for consensus Speak with one voice	Breakthroughs Focus on the future Strategic leadership Generative thinking Learning way forward Bold vision
	Delegating to the organizational leader	*Empowering the organizational leader*	*Charting a new course*
	MICROMANAGEMENT	MICROGOVERNANCE	STATUS QUO GOVERNANCE
LESS EFFECTIVE	Intervening board members Hands-on approach Operational decision making Focus on administrative detail Present-oriented Short-range planning	Policy-fixated board members Reactive Focus on wordsmithing Too little too late Unclear or missing ends policies Confusing limitations policies	Guided by defaults Tweaking the past Change-adverse Focus on maintaining usual state Institutionalized processes Indecisive
	Micromanaging the organizational leader	*Paper handcuffs for the organizational leader*	*Don't rock the boat*

© James C. Galvin, 2020.

to delegate management and not get involved in operational decisions. Navigating boards need people with experience in the area of service or ministry, retired organizational leaders, and people with expertise in the sector.

Different focus: Managing boards focus on making operational decisions and setting guidelines to move the organization forward. Governing boards focus on establishing policies to set strategic direction and set boundaries for the staff. Navigating boards focus on what is changing in the relevant environment. They act to respond to new opportunities or adjust the organizational mission, purpose, recipients, programs, or services for long-range viability.

Different levels: Managing boards delegate tasks, projects, and specific responsibilities to the organizational leader or even to certain staff. They actively track execution on these items. Governing boards delegate management to the organizational leader. If they have any concerns about how things are being done, they express these as limitations policies all written in the negative to avoid interfering with management. Navigating boards delegate governance, either by forming a committee to handle this work, or by spending the least amount of time possible on it. If a board is about to make sweeping changes in an organization, it doesn't matter if the budget is a little off or if the policy manual is not perfect.

Different tools: Boards use tools to do their job. Managing boards develop operating procedures captured in an organizational handbook. This document sets forth how things are to be done at this organization. They also use the budget report as a tool to manage. Governing boards focus on establishing board policies. These policies, captured in a board policy manual, address what is out of bounds for the organizational leader and staff rather than telling them what to do. They also specify the outcomes the organization should strive to achieve. Navigating boards focus on the preferred future of the organization. When they sense major change in the relevant environment, they assess organizational strengths, assets, and what is changing outside of the organization. They determine what is needed now and how the organization must change.

WHICH TYPE OF BOARD IS RIGHT FOR YOUR ORGANIZATION?

Managing, governing, and navigating are all valid options. All three allow a board to fulfill its basic responsibilities. Robert T. Ingram, author of BoardSource's all-time best-selling book, has described ten basic responsibilities of nonprofit boards.

1. Determine mission and purpose
2. Select the chief executive
3. Support and evaluate the chief executive
4. Ensure effective planning
5. Monitor and strengthen programs and services
6. Ensure adequate financial resources
7. Protect assets and provide financial oversight
8. Build a competent board
9. Ensure legal and ethical integrity
10. Enhance the organization's public standing

Managing, governing, and navigating boards all fulfill these basic responsibilities, but in different ways.

What is best depends on your organization and the relevant environment. According to the National Center for Charitable Statistics, there are over 1.5 million nonprofit organizations registered in the US. The most common type is the managing board. This is simply because many of these nonprofits have no paid staff, so they cannot delegate management. The next most common type is the governing board. This has been popularized by the writings of John Carver and others as policy-based governance. The least known is the navigating board, which has been described by Ram Charan, Richard Chait, and others as boards that go beyond writing policies and monitoring performance.

The next three chapters detail how to decide what your organization needs and how to be effective when adopting any of these three types.

CHAPTER 4

MANAGING BOARDS

DEFINITION: A managing board is a group of people who oversee an organization and focus on making decisions about how the organization will operate and what it accomplishes. They tend to reserve important decisions for themselves and delegate smaller operational decisions to the organizational leader and staff. In terms of the black box metaphor, the board oversees the box, opens the lid, looks inside, and works to improve how the organization is functioning. This can be done effectively or ineffectively.

This type of board is also called a working board or a traditional board. Working board means there are no paid staff in the organization and the board must make the decisions and then do all the work. A traditional board is a generic term to refer to how a board with staff usually functions without the discipline of policy-based governance. They involve themselves in operational decisions and developing operating procedures in order to manage the organization. They vote to approve proposals and requests brought forward by the organizational leader.

Many board consultants will directly teach or imply that policy-based governance is the best option of governance for all nonprofit boards. The problem with this viewpoint is that many nonprofit boards do not have the requisite resources in place to implement policy-based governance. If an organization is volunteer-based and has no paid staff, they simply cannot function as a governing board. Or if a nonprofit has an organizational leader who is not fully competent in managing the work, they cannot safely delegate authority to the leader. They must function as a managing board because there is no one else capable of managing the organization to the standard they desire. For these boards, policy-based governance is out of reach.

For a new start-up organization with no staff in place, or only a brand-new organizational leader, the new board will almost certainly begin functioning as a managing board. For an organization like a homeowner's association board, which has paid, professional, outsourced staff, the board must make almost all decisions involved with spending money or making changes in the community.

WHO AND WHAT IS INVOLVED?

Managing boards need people who are elected or invited to serve who have management skills. Managing boards do well with people who like to solve problems and make decisions. They need people who can work together well as a high-performing management team.

They need board members who have C-suite skills. Like any large company, managing boards need people with expertise in operations, finance, human resources, and marketing. Nonprofit organizations would naturally add fundraising expertise to this list.

For recruiting new board members, they would look for people who are experienced managers, administrators, or people with valuable professional skills such as lawyers, accountants, or financial advisors.

They would look for people who own their own businesses or work as a middle manager in a larger firm. They want people who would embody what is found on an effective executive team. To be effective, they might stay away from front-line supervisors and professionals who work independently. They want board members with a higher-level management perspective and experience.

Tools that managing boards use include an annual plan for the organization, an annual budget, meeting minutes, and an operations handbook. The operations handbook is the place where the board and staff capture the standard operating procedures for the organization. Sometimes the personnel policies are included in this handbook and sometimes they are captured in a separate employee handbook.

WHAT IS THE PURPOSE OF THIS BOARD?

A managing board serves as the main decision-making body for the organization. Working together with the organizational leader, they oversee operations and control finances. They essentially supervise the organizational leader. As a group, they make major decisions, approve or reject proposals brought by the organizational leader, delegate authority for certain areas of responsibility, and delegate all day-to-day decisions to the organizational leader.

If the board has a competent organizational leader in place, they can delegate most operating decisions to that person while keeping watch over finances and organizational health. If the board has a weak organizational leader, then they must step in to fill the gaps in performance, whether it means setting annual goals, developing the budget, resolving staff conflict, or any other area of management. The goal is to ensure that the organization is being well-managed.

HOW DOES THIS TYPE OF BOARD WORK?

In meetings, a managing board tends to get involved in operational matters and reserves all the "big decisions" for themselves. Desiring to be a good management team, they go over budget reports in detail, dig into any problems or issues the organization is experiencing, and looks for ways to contribute to the organization by giving suggestions for improvement.

Managing boards tend to meet monthly, but some meet quarterly. If a board does not have a written board policy manual, it will tend to default toward behaving like a managing board.

Regarding number of board members, managing boards can be small, medium, or large. Small boards will tend to function like any management team. Large boards will tend to structure itself with permanent committees to break down the work of management. They may have committees for areas such as finance, human resources, properties, long-range planning, or fundraising. They will usually also have an executive committee because medium to large-sized boards will have difficulty deliberating together in a productive way with so many people around the table.

WHEN IS THIS THE BEST ALTERNATIVE?

Between the three types of boards, the managing board is the best alternative if the organization has no organizational leader, a part-time leader, a weak leader, or nobody else capable of overseeing operations appropriately.

By far, most new start-up nonprofits begin with a board functioning in management mode. The board members are usually passionate about the mission and the new organization. They want to help the organization get off to a good start. Only a few years later as the organization matures do they realize that they must move to a governing mode.

Many small, nonprofit organizations function best with a managing board. Often, the only qualified leader they can find has great passion for the work but does not have all the skills required to manage a nonprofit. Usually, the nonprofit cannot afford to hire all the expertise needed to round out the staff team. The board then needs to step in and assist the organizational leader where needed. This is common for smaller organizations. Larger organizations can afford to add staff to cover any areas of weakness.

Typically, when an organizational leader departs or retires from a nonprofit, the board will seek a replacement from within the organization. This assures that the new organizational leader understands the organizational culture and has a deep knowledge of the work. But often, the person promoted has passion for the mission but does not possess all the skills needed. Most of the paid staff in any nonprofit joined the organization because of the work, the cause, and the mission.

For example, let's say a youth-serving organization that employs a dozen youth workers needs to find a new organizational leader. The board will sometimes offer the position to one of the existing staff. However, that person may be reluctant to take the position because he or she signed up to work with youth, not the board, not donors, and not to supervise other staff. Let's say one of the youth workers who is respected by the other staff reluctantly agrees to take on the new position of organizational leader. That person will need some time to grow into the role. That person will need extra support from the board. This situation will require the board to step in and assist the new leader in certain areas. He or she will need coaching from the board or someone else outside the organization.

Managing mode is also useful for nonprofits that have become rundown or gotten into financial trouble. Due to poor leadership, they have gotten off track and need to get back to basics, terminate low performers, focus on the fundamentals, or rebuild their donor base. But if new competition has arisen, or a shift has occurred in the relevant environment making them obsolete, merely getting back to basics will not save the organization.

Managing mode is not a good fit if a nonprofit has a highly skilled, experienced leader or is a large, complex organization. For example, community hospitals are complex organizations. Board members are often selected from the surrounding community. Sometimes, the only qualification hospital board members possess is that they have been to the doctor. Large, complex organizations need boards that operate in the governing mode and delegate management to the professional staff.

WHAT IS EFFECTIVE?

A managing board that is effective will open the lid of the black box carefully when they meet to avoid unintentionally making things worse for the organization. They will ask questions but avoid unnecessary intervention. They will attempt to be proactive and not reactive as they make decisions.

The ideal for them is to function like the high-level executive team of a business or large nonprofit organization. As a team, they make key decisions together as a group. They want to stay focused on organizational performance rather than organizational processes. They want to delegate skillfully and avoid micromanagement.

Skillful delegation to the organizational leader involves clearly explaining 1) the context of the delegation, 2) the desired end result, 3) the specific assignment or project, 4) any key measures of effectiveness, 5) level of authority for making decisions, 6) support the board will provide, and 7) how to keep the board informed.

For example, suppose a managing board decides to try hosting a special banquet to raise up new donors, something their organizational leader has never organized before. Suppose the board does not want to coordinate the banquet through a committee and feels that the organizational leader is up to the task. Instead of telling the leader how to organize the banquet, they could delegate skillfully in the following way. 1) Point out that the donor base of the organization is growing older and the mailing list is getting smaller. 2) Describe the desired result of a successful banquet that generates new donors excited about supporting the work. 3) Ask the leader to plan and coordinate the new banquet. 4) Set targets such as at least 200 attendees, $10,000 in donations, and over 100 new giving units. 5) Explain that the leader will have a budget of $10,000 to coordinate the event and full authority to set the date, rent the banquet space, and determine all the details of the program. 6) Let the organizational leader know the board will be available as individuals to offer feedback or advice on any aspect of the banquet if asked and will willingly serve as volunteers at the event. 7) Request that the leader email a short report on progress every two weeks from now until the event happens. Then the board should simply stay out of the way.

Sometimes the board must step into operations. For example, if the organizational leader is a person who tends to focus on day-to-day operations and has a difficult time with long-range planning, the managing board will need to assist the organizational leader with strategic thinking, and possibly even with setting annual goals. After all, in some nonprofits if the board did not do it, then nobody would.

Suppose a mid-sized congregation has a single board structure with a pastor who is a warm person and an exceptional counselor, but not gifted at leadership, management, or administration. Let's assume that he never balances his personal checkbook. Short of hiring a business manager or calling a new pastor, this board will be forced to open the black box and fill in the gaps of leadership. An effective board in this situation, will meet with the pastor regularly, carefully monitor the budget reports, discuss tactics for achieving ministry goals, but stop short of telling the pastor how to do his job. Every board meeting can present tempting situations for middle managers and professionals to get into the weeds.

An effective managing board will tend to want to meet monthly. Typically, their bylaws might specify meeting at least ten times per year. Their meetings will be timed to coincide with the monthly budget reports. A budget is a management tool and they will want to use it to be informed of the financial condition of the organization while avoiding fixating on the details. A few line items with a variance over 100 percent is less significant than a downward trend in income or a dangerously low cash reserve.

To stay at an executive team level as much as possible, the board will want to capture their decisions and concerns by developing standard operating procedures and writing them in an operations handbook. A simple example would be determining regular office hours. This will reduce the number of times a managing board will need to intervene inside the black box or be asked to decide about an inconsequential operational matter.

Managing boards can function effectively or ineffectively.

WHAT IS INEFFECTIVE?

A managing board that cannot avoid micromanaging is almost always ineffective. In fact, the only thing worse than a micromanager is a bunch of micromanagers serving as a board.

Why don't managing boards simply avoid ineffective practices? Because micromanaging is easy and fun! Governing boards also tend to step over the line and dive in with detailed questions about operations. At least governing boards have written policies to keep themselves in check. Managing boards have no clear lines of demarcation. Managing boards, by definition, are actually managing the organization, whether together with the organizational leader or by themselves in authority over the leader.

A board that opens the black box and becomes overly tactical increases the chances of them missing larger, strategic issues. Ineffective boards are usually not talking about how the relevant environment is shifting. They are not wondering how their clients, members, or donors are changing. They just keep looking inside the black box and talking about ways to get the numbers back up.

Another difficulty with managing boards is trying to manage an organization with a group of middle managers who have differing values or approaches. For example, should the nonprofit organization pay their bills 30, 60, or 90 days after receiving the invoice? Should the board conduct annual performance reviews with all staff? The deeper a board delves into operations, the more pronounced the disagreements between themselves become with regard to how things ought to be done.

Managing boards that are too big quickly become dysfunctional. It is common for larger boards to have few members who say nothing at all during their two-day meeting. This is one reason why so many boards use a committee structure. This spreads out the work of managing the organization and allows for smaller groups to make decisions.

When using committees, boards need to make sure that the whole board does not remake the decisions and proposals brought forward. In one new church, a small committee was tasked with researching and proposing the purchase of a lighted sign near the highway. The group did its work and reported back with a specific design. The whole board then asked to see the other alternatives. They discussed the pros and cons extensively as a large group before coming to the same conclusion. What should have taken about five minutes took forty-five minutes.

Executive committees are another way of getting around the dysfunctional aspects of larger boards. The executive committee sets the agenda for the meetings of the larger board and sometimes usurps the authority of the full board. Even if the executive committee is serving ethically, it still leaves a feeling among many board members that some board members are flying business class and the rest are back in coach.

Managing boards also feel the uncertainty of trying to manage an organization by meeting one day a month. They don't have all the information they need, so they often ask to invite one or more key staff members to answer their questions, and in effect, help them manage the organization. This practice weakens the ability of the board to hold the staff accountable and does not allow them the freedom to speak plainly about organizational performance.

Some managing boards meet quarterly or less. This makes effective management even more difficult. If a problem emerges, it can be allowed to fester for three or four months before the board can act. If this kind of a board can stay at the executive team level, it can work.

But no board can micromanage once a quarter without making a mess. Some organizational leaders purposely keep their board members in the dark to reduce their tendency to meddle.

Most managing boards just enjoy the thrill of helping make key decisions for the organization without bothering to capture these decisions or the principles behind them in an operations handbook. Documenting the standard operating procedures for an organization can be a useful contribution. Telling the organizational leader or staff how to do their jobs is not.

Ineffective managing boards can produce a lot of humorous stories. One small church decided they needed to replace their van used for youth and seniors. A board member found a good deal on a white van just coming off lease and proposed that the church buy it. Another board member objected because the van had power windows. He said the church didn't need those fancy extras. The other members replied that they were not paying anything extra for those features because it was a used vehicle. The one board member insisted that they look for a different van to demonstrate that they were being good stewards with the money entrusted to them.

HOW DOES THE LEADER WORK WITH THIS TYPE OF BOARD?

A managing board can be frustrating for an organizational leader to work with. The best approach is to partner with them. Help the board view the organizational leader as a part of the top management team. Keep them informed with relevant information so they can work with you in making wise decisions.

The elegance of working with a policy-based board is that it offers a clear distinction between ends and means, between governance and operations, between board work and staff work. With a managing board, that line is not clear. Effective boards and wise organizational leaders will work to define the line between "big" decisions the board wants to reserve for itself and day-to-day decisions the board wants to delegate. Somebody must draw a line somewhere. Creating a list of who makes what decisions can be helpful to clarify this.

Members of managing boards will often feel a temptation to get into the weeds and micromanage the organization. If a board is moving into micromanaging, the organizational leader can offer to take care of that situation with his or her staff. The board chair or another appointed board member can monitor the level of discussion and bring a board back to a higher level of management behavior.

Capturing operational procedures in an organizational handbook can help a managing board avoid making similar decisions over again. These are like limitations policies except they can be stated either positively or negatively.

HOW DOES A BOARD CHAIR LEAD THIS TYPE OF BOARD?

Chairing this type of board is not easy. The main task is to help the board stay out of the weeds. The board chair must clearly explain the difference between managing and micromanaging. This is difficult and is the reason why many boards are eager to transition to policy-based governance.

The board chair should run the meetings like a high-level management team meeting. The focus should be on results and looking ahead to the future. Conversation should be on the strategic and tactical levels without telling the organizational leader or other staff how to do their jobs.

The emphasis should be on teamwork. The board as a team manages the organization, not individual board members. The board as a team makes key decisions and plans. The board chair should involve the organizational leader and work together with him or her to manage the organization.

When monitoring progress, reviewing the budget, or addressing a problem, individual board members will be quick to drill down, attempt to find the root cause, and suggest corrective actions. The only problem is that this might make matters worse for the organizational leader or staff. Board chairs need to draw a line between what is a board decision and what is a staff decision. If the board identifies a problem, they don't have to find a solution. They can task the organizational leader with coming up with a plan to solve it by the next meeting. Sometimes, though, the organizational leader will want help thinking through how to resolve some particularly sensitive situations.

Develop agendas that help the managing board set goals, track progress, and solve problems. Don't let the board create problems. Stick to big decisions and leave smaller decisions and procedures for the staff to determine. Create a decision-making culture that avoids asking for an exhaustive amount of information and postponing key decisions.

Capture decisions in meeting minutes that clearly describe the action of the board as a group and not opinions of individual board members. As much as possible, translate these decisions into standard operating procedures that will become a part of the operations handbook.

The challenges of chairing meetings of managing boards, reigning in micromanaging board members, and dysfunctional boards unintentionally making matters worse for the organization, make governing boards look quite attractive.

CHAPTER 5

GOVERNING BOARDS

DEFINITION: A governing board is a group of people who oversee an organization and focus on resources going into the organization and results coming out. Rather than making operational decisions, they develop board policies describing desired outcomes to be achieved and staff actions to be avoided. In terms of the black box metaphor, the board leaves the box lid shut, delegates operational authority to the organizational leader, and limits what happens in the box by writing policies that prohibit certain decisions or actions. This can be done effectively or ineffectively.

While a managing board manages the organization, a governing board delegates management and sticks to governing the organization. A governing board does its work by developing policies for the organization that define why the organization exists and empower the organizational leader while holding him or her accountable. This mode is essential when the leader and staff know way more about managing the organization than the board members.

By opening the black box and dabbling in operations, boards can unintentionally make matters worse for the organization. For example, a board that wants to conduct the annual performance review for all key staff members cannot make a sound evaluation without being able to observe these individuals in action at work. Or a church board that wants to set annual goals for worship attendance may not realize that is the wrong measure to use. Many boards will do better if they operate as a governing board and stay out of management.

Many organizations have attempted to transition to policy-based governance and have had a bad experience. This is usually due to botched implementation. One mistake is that boards sit back and stop monitoring organizational health and performance. Another mistake is transitioning without writing any board policies. It is difficult to be policy-based without any written policies, but I have seen a lot of nonprofits try.

WHO AND WHAT IS INVOLVED?

Governing boards need people who want to stick to governing and stay out of management. Governing boards need members who can think strategically, are focused on the future, have a deep passion for the work, are willing to develop written policies, and who are team players.

These represent different skill sets than are desirable for a managing board. A governing board with two accountants, two lawyers, and two of several other types of professionals is called a Noah's ark board. What works for a managing board becomes problematic for a governing board. A larger nonprofit will have a chief financial officer and marketing professionals on staff. If they need help with writing personnel policies, they can hire a human resources consultant. If they need legal advice, they can hire a lawyer. They don't need to load up the board with people who can help them manage the organization.

What larger and more mature nonprofit organizations need is a board that can define why the organization exists, set limits to staff actions, delegate all operations to the organizational leader while holding him or her accountable, and generally oversee the sustainability and performance of the organization.

Governing boards require written board policies captured in a board policy manual. These are not what are often called organizational policies or operational procedures. Board policies are written at the governing level, above and outside of the black box. Anything dealing with how things are done inside the black box are better called standard operating procedures. These are captured by the leader and staff in an operations handbook.

If a board is following the approach developed by John Carver, then they will create four kinds of board policies: Organizational Ends, Executive Limitations, Board-Management Delegation, and Governance Process.

The first section of the board policy manual, organizational ends, will describe why the organization exists. It is concerned with the resources going into the black box and the results coming out the other side. For any nonprofit organization, the results describe how people's lives are being changed, not how much is happening inside the black box.

The second section of the board policy manual will capture limitations policies. Any board wanting to stay out of the black box will be concerned about what is happening inside. They may be concerned about the level of financial reserves, proper maintenance of facilities, or ethical treatment of clients. Rather than attempting to improve operating procedures, which they might be ill-equipped to do, they can set limits on what actions are not allowed in the black box. So, the board policies in this section are written in the negative.

For example, they may specify that the organizational leader may not make an unbudgeted expenditure above $5,000 without board approval.

The third section of the board policy manual will describe the relationship between the board and the organizational leader. The board delegates all management and all operational decisions to the organizational leader. The leader then manages the organization. But the leader is accountable to the board and regularly reports to the board in the way the board requests. The board oversees the organization while staying out of operational decisions and focusing instead on results.

The last section of the board policy manual describes how the board will conduct its work. This will include expectations of individual board members, how the board will function as a group, and anything else about what happens in a board meeting.

Boards can use the name for each section originated by John Carver or an alternative. These sections can be arranged in any order in the board policy manual. An appendix containing other organizational documents can be added. The key is to ensure that the board has at least these four sections and that each section is comprehensive.

We can compare these four sections of the board policy manual to a diagram of a football stadium. The ends policies are like the end zone. This is how the organization scores points. The limitations policies are like the out of bounds line. We want the organizational leader and staff to stay in bounds.

With these two sections of policies, the board has the organization under control. If the organizational leader and staff implement the policies, then the organization will be heading in the right direction and will avoid actions and behaviors the board has prohibited.

After making the ends and limitations clear, the board can then tell

LABEL	SUMMARY
Organizational Ends OR **Desired Outcomes**	Desired outcomes describe the ends or purposes of the organization. Desired outcomes policies, or ends policies, describe what results the organization is here to achieve, who the recipients will be, and the cost of those results. These policies do not address means, methods, activities, or specific programs. Every policy in this section must address either results, recipients, or cost. Desired outcomes reflect the never-ending work of the board in determining what the organization will attempt to accomplish in the future.
Executive Limitations OR **Staff Limitations**	Executive Limitations policies address staff means—what the organizational leader and staff may and may not do. They define the out-of-bounds lines. These policies communicate what behaviors, methods, and practices are acceptable and not acceptable. Unless restricted by the policies, all other reasonable actions are considered acceptable. This approach empowers the staff from needing to delay action until the board can approve each new initiative. It also allows the board to responsibly minimize involvement in the details of day-to-day operations. These policies are addressed to the organizational leader rather than the entire staff. The organizational leader is held accountable that all staff actions fall within the boundaries established by these policies.
Board-Management Delegation OR **Board-Staff Relationship**	Board-Staff Relationship policies address how the board and organizational leader relate to each other. In general, the board speaks with one voice and all board authority is delegated through the organizational leader. This means the organizational leader reports to the board as a whole, not to individual board members, officers of the organization, or board committees. This also means the board works only with the organizational leader and does not direct the work of staff or volunteers.
Governance Process OR **Board Process**	Board process policies describe the standards of behavior for individual board members and the board as a group. These policies describe the way the board operates. They clarify the governing style of the board, role of the board chair, board member conduct, board member responsibilities, and the use of committees. If any board process issue arises that is not specified by these policies, the board chair should guide board process. The board represents and serves the moral owners of the organization.

the organizational leader that any operational decision that is making progress toward the end zone and stays in bounds is automatically pre-approved by the board. This is empowering for the organizational leader and staff. They can move ahead with confidence instead of worrying whether the board will approve of their operational decisions.

Meanwhile, on the stadium diagram, the board is up in the suites. They are up high and can see everything happening on the field. There are some rules about how they behave in the suite, no yelling or swearing for example. These rules are like the board process policies that show us how to do our work.

There is a red phone in the corner of the suite that is connected to the headset of the coach. With this phone the coach calls up with reports on players who are hurt or information about plays he is going to run. He is not asking permission to run the plays, just keeping the board informed. This is like the board-staff relationship policies that show how the board empowers the leader while at the same time holding the leader accountable.

WHAT IS THE PURPOSE OF THIS BOARD?

A governing board is a group that generally oversees an organization for sustainable mission fulfillment. They develop board policies and govern the organization through them. Rather than manage the organization, they hire a competent leader, delegate all management and day-to-day decisions, and hold him or her accountable.

If the board has an organizational leader whose performance is unacceptable, the board has the option of replacing the leader or keeping the leader and tightening staff limitations policies so more operational decisions must be approved by the board. For example, the board may limit unbudgeted expenditures to $1,000 without board approval. Or the board may retain the responsibility of developing a long-range strategic plan rather than delegating it.

HOW DOES THIS TYPE OF BOARD WORK?

The meeting agenda and all reports should be sent to board members before the meeting. All board members should prepare thoroughly. In meetings, a governing board will receive and discuss monitoring reports about the organization at the frequency and in the format they determine.

Budget reports, for example, may be one page in length or extensively detailed. The board determines what level of detail will best give them the information they need to monitor the organization.

If the organizational leader brings a proposal or key decision to the board for approval, the board will first check to see if this is covered by their existing policies. If it is not, they will determine whether a new policy or an adjustment to an existing policy is needed. After the policy change is made, the organizational leader may proceed without approval from the board. Sometimes the organizational leader will bring an issue to the board, the board will discuss it thoroughly, then determine if the existing policy provides adequate guidance for the organizational leader to make the call alone or together with staff.

Governing boards may meet monthly, but some prefer to meet quarterly or two times a year face-to-face. ECFA guidelines specify that boards meet at least three times per year and one of those may be a conference call. If a well-run organization has a highly competent, organizational leader, there is often little reason for governing boards to meet more than four times per year.

Governing boards may be small, medium, or large. If large, they may create a governance committee to draft policies, review every section at least once a year, and keep the board policy manual up to date.

If you compare a nonprofit to a cruise ship, the board represents the owners of the ship. They hire the captain, determine the destination, and maybe have some input on the preferred course. But the board members need to stay out of the engine room.

WHEN IS THIS THE BEST ALTERNATIVE?

When dealing with professionally trained staff, it is extremely difficult for a typical board to supervise them. The board needs to up its game and move from managing mode to governing mode. Then they must develop their board policies and stick to governing.

When dealing with large or complex organizations, like hospitals or universities, functioning in the governing mode is almost mandatory. People selected for university boards may be successful businesspeople, but they usually have no idea what it takes to balance the demands of students, parents, staff, major donors, a unionized faculty, accreditation, and government regulations. Any university board that starts making management decisions for a university is sure to create a mess.

The governing approach will also work with small nonprofits. A local social service agency can be quite complex with professional certifications, government funding of services, writing of grants, and taking legal precautions. Local citizens recruited to serve as a part of this board will usually not have the knowledge or experience to manage the organization or staff adequately.

The governing mode will also work well with fast growing nonprofits that are well-led. It provides a structure that helps the board stay out of the way and allows the staff to manage the rapid growth.

Governing boards can function effectively or ineffectively.

WHAT IS EFFECTIVE?

A governing board that is effective keeps the lid on the black box closed and focuses on the outside of the box: resources going in and results coming out. They hire a competent leader and hold the organizational leader accountable for organizational performance and results. They oversee the organization to ensure good stewardship of all resources, general health of the organization, and effective performance.

Governing boards delegate operational procedures and the operating handbook to the organizational leader and staff. The board focuses on developing governing policies and capturing those in their board policy manual.

Effective governing boards make sure they have compelling ends policies that meet real needs in society. They always state limitations policies in the negative to prohibit actions instead of specifying them, thereby keeping them out of management. They focus on results to be attained and don't tell the organizational leader or staff how to do their jobs.

Effective governing boards review each section of their policy manual at least once a year. They also review their bylaws annually to make sure the board and the organization is remaining in compliance with them.

Effective boards communicate with their constituents, stakeholders, members, or donors to keep them informed and inspire passion for the work.

In general, governing boards will pay more attention to quarterly financial statements than monthly budget reports. A budget is a management tool and extremely useful for the organizational leader and staff for making operational decisions. A governing board ought to be more concerned for the actual financial condition of the organization as opposed to line item budget variances. Quarterly reports tend to even out the blips that show up in monthly reports due to holidays or weather or other seasonal factors.

Effective boards monitor organizational performance closely but are careful to stay on their side of the line. Board members can ask questions about operations but should avoid giving advice. Effective boards refrain from managing and stick to governing.

WHAT IS INEFFECTIVE?

Governing boards can reduce their effectiveness by micromanaging, microgoverning, or becoming passive.

Micromanaging is the most common failure. If the organizational leader brings up an issue the organization is facing, board members who are skilled managers, or who own their own business, want to jump in and fix the problem. They want to drill down and get to the root cause. They are good at this. They are genuinely trying to help. But if the organizational leader does not need or want their help, they are unintentionally making matters worse.

Limitations policies are written in the negative to prevent board members from stepping over the line into management. But some board members want to use limitations policies as a back door into management. For example, a board might have a limitations policy stating that the organizational leader shall not fail to have bathrooms that are fully accessible to young children, handicapped clients, and older adults. That is a perfectly acceptable limitations policy. A limitations policy steps over the line when it states something like this: The organizational leader shall not fail to install Kohler elongated, comfort height toilets, in a white finish, with stainless steel grab bars on both sides of the stall.

For many board members, it is a continuous temptation to open the black box, take a peek, and start making suggestions for improvement. Members of governing boards may be curious but must stay on their side of the line. Boards waste organizational resources when they get in the way.

Microgoverning is being so concerned over the wordsmithing of policies and the polishing of the board policy manual that they lose track of how the organization is performing. Reviewing existing policies and getting them just right tends to be more attractive for some than discussing why charitable gifts are down for the past three years.

Writing excessively restrictive policies result in paper handcuffs for the organizational leader. The purpose of the board is not to write a manual or control details of operations, but to ensure good stewardship of resources and organizational performance.

Sometimes, governing boards become passive. They stop actively monitoring organizational performance and do not inject any new ideas or energy into the organization.

One sign of passivity is when board members neglect preparing for the meeting. If reports are sent out ahead of time, all board members should study these and come prepared with comments and questions. One organization sent all their handouts to board members across the nation at great expense by FedEx. At the beginning of the meeting one of the board members sat down and opened his box for the first time.

Another sign of passivity is board members who make no comments during the meeting. If they have nothing to say for the entire board meeting, it makes one wonder how these individuals got recruited for the board in the first place?

Passive board members do not think ahead, do not initiate new ideas, and do not monitor organizational performance. They are not making a useful contribution to the organization.

HOW DOES THE LEADER WORK WITH THIS TYPE OF BOARD?

If a board implements policy-based governance well, many typical board problems can be avoided, and the board can make a significant contribution as they govern. The biggest temptation for governing board members is a compelling desire to start managing the organization.

A thorough board orientation process can help all new board members get started with the right mindset. With term limits, a board tends to end up with all new members over time who have never had any training in policy-based governance.

Organizational leaders should refrain from asking the board for advice in board meetings. The board will tend to ask for more detail, start problem-solving, and will gladly offer advice. But if a governing board offers advice, does the organizational leader have to take it? An organizational leader should not ask for advice about operational matters. If a board offers advice, the leader can thank them and remind them the decision falls into his or her realm of authority. An organizational leader can always seek advice or counsel from individual board members apart from the board meeting without dragging the board into operations.

HOW DOES A BOARD CHAIR LEAD THIS TYPE OF BOARD?

Chairing this type of board is not easy. The biggest challenge is keeping board members out of staff work and doing board work. Some board chairs pass out red cards that any board member can hold up if a discussion is heading into the weeds. When the indicator is held up, the question can be asked if the board is doing staff work or board work. This technique can be quite effective. No player wants a red card.

To keep a governing board on track, build a solid agenda. The board policies should offer a typical agenda format and a list of tasks to be accomplished at each meeting throughout the year. Combine these two items then talk with the organizational leader. What else does he or she want to include on the agenda. Rule out anything that is a management decision by reminding the leader he or she can simply make that decision and report it to the board later.

Building a solid agenda is not easy. I served on a board where several of the staff would give long, verbal reports on their work. I was getting frustrated because I recommend that most boards do this through written reports ahead of time and all board members should come prepared with questions or comments. Being a consultant, I started to analyze why this kept happening. Then I realized that the typical agenda had never been adjusted. To my horror, I realized this was my fault. I was the board chair and had approved every board meeting agenda the past few years. I was not giving the agenda enough attention. The organizational leader put together a draft of the agenda and emailed it to me based on previous meetings. I quickly looked it over and approved it or added an item or two. I was not spending time crafting the agenda we needed to enhance our performance as a governing board.

Find a way to build cohesive relationships outside of the boardroom. This may be done through sharing meals together or meeting at a retreat location. Grill some steaks in somebody's backyard with board members and spouses. These kinds of relationship-building efforts will form the connective tissue that can keep a governing board working together and helping each other stick to board work.

If the board is having difficulty writing a new limitations policy, ask them to consider what value they are trying to protect. This can help elevate their thinking and create a concise policy that effectively protects the organization.

If any board members are continuously disruptive or rude, deal with the behavior one on one as the board chair. If that does not work, bring it up as a full board discussion. If they refuse to change, ask them to voluntarily step down.

Often, the organizational leader will bring up topics that drag governing boards into management. This is sometimes done by the leader asking for advice on an operational issue. Sometimes it is from excessive operational detail in the leader's report. As the board chair, you want to keep board members focused on what is happening outside the box and not what is happening inside.

Excessive detail in reports reminds me a Jerry Seinfeld joke about riding on a commercial jet. After takeoff, the pilot will sometimes make an announcement giving extreme detail about the cruising altitude and flight plan. Seinfeld said it made him want to walk to the front of the plane, knock on the door, and say, "That's all well and fine. But when you are all done, can you make sure we end up in the place that it says on the ticket?"

The board chair needs to keep the governing board focused on results. In terms of operations, the board chair should use exception reporting, which means the board only talks about what is happening inside of the box if there is a big problem or if a limitations policy is being exceeded.

Turbulent times call for bold action. Sometimes setting policy alone is not enough. That is when navigating boards are needed.

CHAPTER 6

NAVIGATING BOARDS

DEFINITION: A navigating board is a group of people who oversee an organization and focus on what is changing in the environment that has created new opportunities or has impacted the viability of the organization. They tend to ignore what is happening operationally and look for new possibilities and new strategic directions for the organization. In terms of the black box metaphor, they pick up the box and move it to a new location or radically change the shape of the box. This can be done effectively or ineffectively.

While a managing board delegates tasks and projects and a governing board delegates management, a navigating board delegates the work of policy review and writing. They do this by assigning the work to a committee, sometimes called a governance committee, or by setting aside the board policy manual for an extended period. The policies remain in place and in force for governing the organization, but the board spends little or no time refining them.

If a board suddenly jumps in and starts making changes in the processes of an organization or attempts to manage cash flow, they are not navigating, they are managing. They became concerned because of a crisis or something going wrong, and they opened the lid of the black box and started making decisions. Navigating boards leave the lid closed, let the organizational leader continue to manage the organization, and they focus on how the whole organization needs to be reset or repositioned.

Sometimes an organization is running smoothly and is well-managed but the world changes. Consequently, the organization will need to be repositioned or repurposed.

WHO AND WHAT IS INVOLVED?

Navigating boards need people with deep knowledge about the social context the organization is operating in. These boards need people who have experienced major change initiatives or been a part of mergers or acquisitions. They need wise people unafraid of making disruptive decisions for the sake of the cause. These boards are more like a brain trust or turnaround team than a traditional governing board. They can offer powerful, strategic insights to the organizational leader.

Compare this to a technology company that promotes one of their staff, who is 45 years old, to the CEO position. The board is packed with retired executives who used to run companies like this one or who are industry veterans with deep knowledge of what it takes to compete and succeed. These board members were brought on for their expertise. They come prepared to work together to shape the company to succeed in a competitive and fast-changing environment. This company, with a new CEO in an ultra-competitive industry, needs a navigating board.

Navigating boards tend to work better when they have fewer board members. Larger boards will have difficulty coming to consensus about making major shifts in an organization they care about. Sometimes, new board members with experience in navigating turbulent environments will need to be recruited.

If a board cannot easily find these kind of board members or does not control who is elected to the board, another option is for the board to appoint a committee to do the navigating work. Or they can appoint a special task force of external people with the wisdom and life experience to study what the organization is facing and recommend the changes that must happen.

The most helpful tool for a navigating board is a strategic map. This is a diagram that highlights the challenges and strategic options for moving forward. These can be quite creative. Physical maps help travelers navigate water, terrain, or highways. Another tool is an opportunity audit, which is a list of potential new ventures, new services, or new markets the board could pursue. Consider what kind of diagram will help the board sum up where it is at and point out options for moving forward.

WHAT IS THE PURPOSE OF THIS BOARD?

A navigating board is a group that reinvents or repurposes an organization to seize new opportunities or to secure organizational survival. They may adjust the target audience, move to new locations, change the organizational mission, search for new funding sources, switch to a new business model, ask for new approaches to serve clients, narrow product offerings, go digital, merge with another nonprofit, or mandate an orderly shutdown.

This type of board moves from generally overseeing an organization and holding the organizational leader accountable, to becoming a change agent for securing the future. They look at what is changing in the relevant environment and attempt to make sense of it. If the organization is heading for a cliff, the board needs to intervene and work closely with the organizational leader to make the major adjustments needed. If the leader strongly opposes these actions of the board, then they need to find a new leader.

HOW DOES THIS TYPE OF BOARD WORK?

A navigating board may start out as a managing or governing board. If the organization experiences a sudden shift in its relevant environment, it may cause new opportunities to emerge, or reveal an eminent threat. This may motivate the board to become proactive in seizing the opportunity, mitigating the threat, or adjusting to the changing context. They must let go of managing and policy-making for a season to focus on how the organization needs to change.

Depending on the individual who is serving as the leader of the organization, the navigating board can approve the staff plans, co-create the plans with the organizational leader, or guide the major changes and strategic shifts from the boardroom.

Some board members, who are averse to making major changes to an organization they love, may feel compelled to leave the board. Others may be upset at how the world is changing but want to leave the organization as unchanged as possible. This often produces conflict between the members who see the changes in the environment and the need to make major adjustments, and the ones who downplay the changes and determine the staff just have to try harder to make it work.

As the relevant environment slowly shifts for every nonprofit, there are times when the organizational leader or board senses a strategic inflection point that requires major adjustments on the part of the organization. The path forward may seem messy or unclear. During these times, a governing board is inadequate. The new path forward often requires a total rewrite of the ends policies or desired outcomes of an organization.

Suppose a small organization pioneered a new model for mentoring at-risk youth. They were able to recruit adults and train them effectively to make a positive difference in the life of a teenager. They were warmly welcomed in the neighborhoods where they served. After five years, they were able to document significant positive outcomes in the lives of the mentees. Then, a foundation heard about their new methods and extraordinary results and offered a large grant over several years to scale their program nationally. But their founder and organizational leader does not have the skills or vision to grow the organization. What should the board do? Should they turn down the grant? Should they force out the founder? Should they launch a separate national organization?

Consider the board of an orphanage in the 1960s. Though they received no government funding, they suddenly saw themselves going out of business because the state where they were located shifted to a foster care system. They had plenty of charitable donations but no access to children in need. What should the board do? Should they become a placement agency for the state foster care system? Should they remodel their building and lease it as low-cost office space for other nonprofits? Should they shut down or adapt in another way?

What if a small nonprofit had a thriving ministry with high school students in Bible quizzing. They had wired benches, a big scoreboard, and hosted an annual state tournament. But then, in the 1970s, youth culture and youth ministry radically changed. Churches suddenly stopped participating in their programs. What should the board do? Target a younger audience? Minister to youth in a different way with unskilled staff? Wait a few decades until Bible quizzing becomes in fashion once again? Should they shut down or adapt in some other way?

These are the kinds of situations that require a board to transition to navigating mode. Discussing agenda items in a routine board meeting make no sense when the organization is facing these kinds of challenges. If the staff cannot or will not adapt, the board must take action.

WHEN IS THIS THE BEST ALTERNATIVE?

A navigating board is the best alternative when exciting new opportunities have emerged or when something has changed in the relevant environment that significantly decreases the effectiveness of the organization. In other words, when the long-term viability of the black box is in doubt. This is the best alternative for any board when something must change, and the sooner the better.

The organization does not necessarily have to be in crisis. For example, it could be using an approach to its work that is no longer producing the results it once did, but funding from their donor base is still going strong. Existing staff can be strongly embracing their outmoded methods and happy to keep doing their work the way they have always done it. Or, it could be sensing an entirely new opportunity that has opened for the organization. Only the board is concerned about how the relevant environment has changed and sensing the adjustments to the organization that must be made.

Positive changes in the relevant environment might also trigger a shift to navigating mode. For example, if a metropolitan area becomes a new site for settling foreign refugees, a social service agency may have a new population to serve and plentiful funding sources. Or another similar agency may shut its doors leaving a segment of the population suddenly underserved.

Every organization will have its board shift to a navigating mode at some point in its organizational lifecycle. This can happen when an organization has been plateaued for years and a substantial shift in the environment has just occurred, when an organization is in significant decline because of mismatch with its context, or when an organization is forced to shut down because of a lack of cashflow or relevance.

Navigating boards can function effectively or ineffectively.

WHAT IS EFFECTIVE?

A navigating board is at its best when it ignores what is happening inside the black box, leaves the lid shut, and examines how the relevant environment has changed. They look at what the world needs now and what the existing organization could possibly offer. They look at how potential clients and members have changed and how the way the organization does its work needs to adjust. They look for new opportunities that are emerging.

For example, Christian camps used to provide an attractive alternative to a long, boring summer for most children and youth in the 1960s and 1970s. Fifty years later, society changed. Children have video games and cell phones. Sports leagues practice and compete year-round. Many youths are over-programmed. Traditional summer camps have stiff competition. If a camp can't compete, it must adjust. Spending more money on rebranding and marketing materials will not solve the problem because the relevant environment has shifted. If a camp is headed for financial disaster, the board needs to shift to a navigating mode and put all the options on the table.

Navigating boards are effective when they research root causes, work together with the organizational leader, involve existing staff to the extent possible, communicate with donors and other stakeholders, brainstorm radical options, and make bold moves.

When working with organizations attempting to find a new, breakthrough strategy, I find that going back to the organization's founding and history can offer important clues for moving forward. The organization's "creation story" may offer seeds of hope. Why was this organization started in the first place? What was the need it met? What benefits did it bring to people? What has changed in the relevant environment?

Looking back to major adjustments an organization has made in its past can also be instructive and encouraging. Usually, methods and programming have had to change many times over its decades of existence. The current situation is another of that type of challenge. It is good to remind staff and donors that the organization has made major adjustments in the past and can successfully make major adjustments again.

Navigating boards are effective when they remain in navigating mode until the major change initiatives are completed and the organization has established a new normal. They must solidify the adjustments in purpose and programming and stabilize as an organization or start on a new growth curve. At that point, the board can move back to managing or governing mode.

WHAT IS INEFFECTIVE?

During turbulent times, ineffective boards move into navigating mode for the purpose of maintaining the status quo. They want to get things back to the way they were as soon as possible. They will initiate major fundraising efforts in order to prop up an increasingly irrelevant organization. They will tend to dismiss new competition in their space.

As an example, consider how the railroad companies ignored trucks as competition in the 1940s. In the beginning, trucks were not that large and there was no Interstate highway system. Later, semi-trucks were built that could transport significant amounts of cargo more flexibly than trains. Eventually, the railroad companies realized the relevant environment had shifted for them and they were in trouble.

Less effective boards will neglect governing policies altogether rather than keeping them in force but assigning that work to a committee or spending minimal time on that work.

Less effective boards will tend to tweak existing strategy rather than make the major adjustments needed. They will not look deeply at what is changing in the relevant environment or why it is occurring. They vaguely realize they are on a sinking ship, yet they don't want to rock the boat.

HOW DOES THE LEADER WORK WITH THIS TYPE OF BOARD?

If a board senses a need to be more proactive and shift into navigating mode, the organizational leader needs to shift with them and become a full partner with the board. The organizational leader must investigate what shifts are occurring in the environment and learn together with the board.

Some board members will be drawn to managing or micromanaging. The organizational leader will need to engage the board in generative and strategic conversations without inviting them into management. The board needs to keep the lid of the black box closed and focus on the driving forces acting on the organization.

These changes can be positive, such as when new opportunities emerge for the organization. When a board is talking about the relative merit of new opportunities, they are not doing management work. When they decide the organization should pursue a new opportunity, then the organizational leader can offer to handle implementation to keep the board out of management work.

HOW DOES A BOARD CHAIR LEAD THIS TYPE OF BOARD?

Chairing this type of board is not easy. It involves a shift from being a board refraining from interfering in management to becoming one that is moving the organization to a new place. Any board chair will probably encounter significant resistance to this shift from generally overseeing to mandating major modifications. This includes the criticism that the board chair is violating policy-based governance and intervening inappropriately. Technically, the board is not opening the lid of the black box and making managerial changes. The board is adjusting the overall inputs, processes, and intended outputs for a better match with the relevant environment.

This can be quite frustrating for a board chair. If operating in governing mode, the most frequent complaint from some board members is that they are not allowed to make decisions and act. But when a sudden environmental shift happens, the main complaint is that the board is violating policy-based governance. Again technically, the board is not violating policy-based governance, but rather picking up the black box and moving it to a better place or reshaping it in a significant way.

Keep the board externally focused. Don't worry about current management or underperforming programs. Some of those managers and programs may not be a part of the future of the organization. Don't worry about fine-tuning governing policies. The board will have time to refine those when they successfully emerge from the other side of the change.

Urge the board members to engage with you in generative thinking and fresh vision for the future. Brainstorm as many potential directions as you can. The board will have time to deliberate on the pros and cons of each as they go. Lead them to think strategically together rather than do strategic planning.

When the board decides to act, make bold moves. Don't tinker. Carefully consider the timing of announcements to staff, donors, and other constituencies.

As a group, the board should take the posture of learning their way into the future. Obtain staff input for new ideas. Run quick tests and pilot groups. Experiment with new approaches. Use flexible planning and emergent strategy. No one board member will likely know what to do. The organizational leader will not likely know what to do. But as a group, the organizational leader and navigating board can find a path forward.

CHAPTER 7

MAKING A TRANSITION

Learning about these three types of boards will make many board chairs, board members, and organizational leaders wonder where their board is at and where they should be for optimum performance.

Given the three types of boards, there are several possible transitions to help a board become more effective. They can move from micromanagement to executive management, from microgovernance to policy-based governance, from status quo governance to transformative governance, from managing mode to governing mode, or governing mode to navigating mode. Moving up means increasing in board effectiveness, while moving sideways means changing the governing mode.

To make a transition, identify as a board where you currently are and where you want to be.

	MANAGING	GOVERNING	NAVIGATING
	EXECUTIVE MANAGEMENT	POLICY-BASED GOVERNANCE	TRANSFORMATIVE GOVERNANCE
MORE EFFECTIVE			
	MICROMANAGEMENT	MICROGOVERNANCE	STATUS QUO GOVERNANCE
LESS EFFECTIVE			

When a new nonprofit is established, it usually launches with a managing board. As the organization matures and competent leadership is hired, the board may feel the need to upgrade its performance and move to policy-based governance. If new opportunities emerge, or if the relevant environment shifts to make the organization becomes less effective or less sustainable, then the board may decide to shift into navigating mode to chart a new course forward. However, a nonprofit may open with a board operating in governing or navigating mode as well.

No board can easily shift from managing mode to navigating mode because they need to have governing policies in place first. Part of the definition of the navigating mode is delegating governance. If the board is in managing mode, this implies they have nobody to hand off the management to in order to be in navigating mode. As a group, a board can't be primarily focused on what is happening inside the box as well as focused on the relevant environment. Pressing organizational issues will always feel more urgent and demand more attention than the slow-moving or distant driving forces outside the organization.

Here are guidelines for making a transition and common pitfalls to avoid.

MICROMANAGEMENT TO EXECUTIVE MANAGEMENT

The basic move here is to help board members stay out of the weeds. Any board that determines it should be a managing board should attempt to function like a high-level executive team. Effective management teams avoid micromanagement. They tend to delegate day-to-day operating decisions and stick with strategic issues. Like owning a minimart, the managing board will want to retain an owner's mindset rather than a manager's mindset.

Reports: Managing boards should specify what kind of reports they want from the organizational leader and at what level of detail. This will help them feel informed without having to grill the organizational leader with an abundance of questions during the board meetings.

Orientation: Managing boards should be proactive, not reactive. Board members should avoid criticizing the organizational leader over a decision that has already been made or money that has already been spent. The board can't change what has happened. Instead, the board should focus on the future and what can be influenced currently.

Delegation: Managing boards should use skillful delegation when handing off projects or major areas of responsibility to the organizational leader. When delegating any responsibility, a board should clarify the level of authority the organizational leader possesses to make decisions during implementation. Governing boards are handing off nearly full authority while managing boards are handing off smaller, more tightly defined responsibilities.

Red line: Managing boards clearly define what decisions are within the realm of the board and what decisions are delegated to the organizational leader. Some decisions will need to be made by the board and organizational leader together. Create a chart that clarifies who makes what decisions, then ask the board to stay on their side of the line.

	LEADER	TOGETHER	BOARD
Draft strategic plan			
Approve strategic plan			
Draft annual operating plan			
Approve annual operating plan			
Draft operating procedures			
Approve operating procedures			
Propose budget			
Approve budget			
Control cash flow			

Hire staff			
Manage staff			
Conduct performance evaluations			
Evaluate program effectiveness			

Partnership: As much as possible, the organizational leader and managing board should commit to working together closely to resolve problems, improve processes, overcome challenges, and ensure that the organization will be sustainable and increasingly effective.

MICROGOVERNANCE TO POLICY-BASED GOVERNANCE

The basic move here is to help the board to govern well. There are two ways to go wrong in with this type of board. One is for board members to become fixated on details of policy writing. The other is for board members to become passive and increasingly disengaged in the work of governing.

Engagement: Increase board member engagement by reviewing board member expectations listed in the board policy manual, asking for renewed commitment at the beginning of each year, and thanking individual board members for their efforts.

Preparation: Send out all written reports ahead of time and ask all board members to review the materials thoroughly and come prepared to ask questions in the meeting.

Agenda: The board chair and organizational leader should work together to craft the agenda for each meeting. After opening items such as approving the agenda, approving the past minutes, and receiving reports, place the strategic items early in the agenda and leave administrative or less important items for later in the meeting.

Utilization: A common error is for a board to transition to policy-based governance, develop its board policy manual, then neglect to refer to their own policies. When meeting together they continue to function in managing mode. It's not enough for a board to call itself policy-based, and it's not enough for a board to have a written board policy manual. They must use their policies to be effective.

Ends: Focus more on ends policies and progress toward organizational results rather than operational matters. Spend time on strategic discussions about how the organization intends to accomplish its desired outcomes.

Limitations: Some board members like to spend inordinate amounts of time detailing limitations policies as a back door to controlling operations. Instead of making long, bulleted lists of behaviors that the board wants to limit, start with the value the board is trying to protect. Once this is stated, the more detailed lists sometimes become less necessary.

Nesting: Board policy manuals can become unnecessarily long and complicated over time. Maintain the policy writing discipline of starting with the highest-order policy first, then moving down one level at a time. Be sure to use full sentences and avoid skipping levels.

Review: Every board should review each section of their board policy manual and their bylaws once a year. This may be done all in one meeting or one section at a time. Board members should review each section prior to the meeting noting improvements to be made.

Education: The board chair should ensure that the board receives ongoing governance training. This can be accomplished by reading a book together or using online resources. It could also involve inviting guest presenters from the larger community.

STATUS QUO GOVERNANCE TO TRANSFORMATIVE GOVERNANCE

The basic move here is to help the organization exploit a new opportunity, make major changes, or adapt to a shifting environment. Instead of trying to get things back to normal, an effective navigating board makes bold moves to help establish a new normal.

The natural tendency of any nonprofit organization will be to attempt to maintain its current equilibrium rather than introduce disruptive adaptations. Status Quo boards sometimes make it worse by trying to hold on to the past and even preventing change. They will get involved in fundraising activities to prop up the organization, maintain traditions, and postpone what might be inevitable.

Urgency: Emphasize what is changing in the relevant environment that needs to be addressed. Explore a range of plausible scenarios of what the organization may face soon. Point out that current opportunities can quickly disappear.

Learning: As a board, learn your way into the future together. Start by admitting that nobody knows what is going to happen in the organization's relevant environment. Then keep observing, keep reading, and keep discussing together what is changing outside the organization.

Innovation: Ask for bold thinking, fresh vision, and creative responses. Run experiments with new ways to do programming and fundraising.

Courage: Don't just tweak what was done in the past. Continuous improvement is good, but it will not resolve new challenges and threats appearing in the relevant environment. Sometimes a board needs to make bold moves.

Traditions: Don't yearn for the good old days when an organization is in decline. At its founding, the organization was a creative response to a need in the world. What does the world need now and what can be the creative response?

MANAGING MODE TO GOVERNING MODE

The basic move here is to delegate the management function and all operational decisions to the organizational leader and raise your game to the governing level. This is done by developing board policies and generally overseeing the organization.

This transition is most useful for larger, more complex nonprofits. If a board has hired professional staff and a competent leader, they will know more about how to manage the organization than the board will. Policy-based governance helps a board to become disciplined at governing well.

This transition can be difficult. Board members who are naturally skilled at management find this change in mode of operation uncomfortable. If not done well, it could leave the organization worse off with weaker accountability.

Any nonprofit organization needs to have four prerequisites in place for a successful transition. These four are 1) a competent leader, 2) board members who want to govern, 3) board members who will stay out of management, and 4) someone with significant governance experience.

A competent leader: No board can transition to policy-based governance without a competent leader the board can trust to do a good job. It is foolish to delegate all operational authority to someone who is unable to handle it. At some point, lack of results will make the selection error painfully obvious. That leaves the board with two choices: hire a new organizational leader or become a managing board.

Board members who want to govern: No board can transition to policy-based governance without board members who are willing to do the tedious work of writing board policies and monitoring performance. Board meetings are extremely boring activities for some people. Passion for the mission of the organization leads them to want to be actively involved in other ways. Somebody must do the hard work of governing.

Board members who will stay out of operations: No board can transition to policy-based governance without board members who will refrain from getting involved with staff work. For gifted managers, management is an enjoyable task. They naturally want to drill down, find the root cause, and fix problems. But a good governing board will avoid getting into detailed, operational matters.

Someone with significant governance experience: No board can transition to policy-based governance without at least one board member with significant experience using policy-based governance. If no one has the expertise, a consultant can assist with this prerequisite. The organizational leader cannot usually lead the board through this transition. In a church, the pastor cannot readily lead the congregation through a change in governance. The organizational leader can provide books and articles to the board members to read until they feel ready to make the transition. If no one on the board is comfortable leading the transition, then the board can hire an outside resource person to assist.

Not every board is ready for policy-based governance. In general, the larger the nonprofit or the more complex its work, the more it's needed. Just don't proceed without the necessary conditions for success in place.

Every organization must make adaptations to structure or process, applying the principles of governance to their unique context. But it is wise to avoid hybrid structures.

Instead of a single board structure, a hybrid model is any situation where a lower-level board is reporting to a higher-level board, or where two or three boards of equal authority are supposed to coordinate. For example, a church with a school might have one board for the church and another for the school. Or a church may have a business board and an elder board. Hybrid structures usually create a myriad of opportunities for conflict between the boards.

One congregation transitioned from a collection of committees to a single board structure using policy-based governance. But they had significant resistance from the existing properties committee. So, they left that group intact and moved to a single board with a separate properties board working alongside of them. It so happened that several of the long-time members were on the properties board and liked making decisions about capital expenditures like spending money on reroofing the church and repaving the parking lot. These spending decisions put the two boards in continual conflict. To finally resolve the problem, they changed the authority level of the properties board to a committee that was advisory only.

GOVERNING MODE TO NAVIGATING MODE

The basic move here is to delegate governance, or limit the time the board spends on it, and focus on what is changing in the relevant environment. This is perhaps the most difficult shift to understand of any of the others previously described.

Shifting to this mode is all about paying attention to what is changing in the relevant environment, and how the organization needs to capitalize on new opportunities or to reinvent or repurpose the organization for survival. It is about picking up the black box and moving it or changing the shape of it in some significant way. Organizations operating in a stable environment rarely need a navigating board. Organizations operating in a turbulent environment or in periods of paralyzing uncertainty usually do.

This pivot to a navigating board will likely last until the turbulence in the environment has subsided or until the organization has found a way to move forward and remain sustainable.

Focus: Rather than focusing on the organization, focus on the immediate contextual factors impacting the organization as well as the larger environmental forces that may have a huge impact soon.

Expertise: Get outside counsel and expertise to help the board understand how these economic and societal changes may occur. Bring on new board members who have weathered similar storms in other organizations.

Meaning: Trends and uncertainties in the environment can lead to strategic confusion. Help board members see meaning in what is happening in society and with potential clients and donors. Be a meaning maker for the organization and its stakeholders.

Scenarios: Use scenario planning as a tool to deal with critical uncertainties. Paint several pictures of how the future may unfold and how the organization can be ready for any of them.

Generativity: As a board, fulfill your fiduciary duties quickly and spend more time in generative thinking. Ask questions like what is trying to happen through us? What new thing is trying to emerge here?

After the crisis is averted and the organization has successfully adapted to the new reality, the board can shift back into a governing mode.

This raises the question about how often boards should consider changing their mode.

FLUIDITY

Which boards should consider making one of these transitions? Every board should be attempting to move from less effective to more effective no matter which type of board they are. But transitioning from one type to another type should be done cautiously and infrequently.

The three types of boards are not fluid states where a board can be managing in one meeting and governing in another. Simply paying attention to the environment and external forces acting upon the organization does not make any group a navigating board. These shifts can happen slowly or quickly, but boards usually stick with one type for a long time.

If a managing board wants to transition to a governing mode, they should be fully committed to it for the long-term future. They should not be dipping back into managing mode unless the organization is being mismanaged or the organization has no leader. To be effective at governing, any board will need to delegate management. If it can't, it will be forced to move back into managing mode. Organizations in significant decline may, at some point, need to right size their governance back to a managing board because a competent leader is no longer in place.

If a governing board transitions to navigating mode, it should be because it is being forced to and may want to transition back to governing as soon as it is able. If a navigating board successfully reinvents or repurposes the organization and a new normal is established, then it can easily shift back into governing mode because they have written policies in place. The ends policies will most likely need to be modified. The limitations policies might need to be adjusted due to new areas of concern for the board. But they should not transition back to governing mode until the new normal is firmly established.

Adaptive governance means a board can shift to a different mode when needed. Any of the three types of boards can become less effective easily by doing what is natural and letting inertia kick in. Each type of board needs to be disciplined in the work it must do.

CHAPTER 8

THE BOARD'S ROLE IN STRATEGY

If you ask directly, many nonprofit leaders will have a difficult time articulating their organization's strategy. They often react by reciting their mission statement. But the mission of the organization is not the same as the strategy for moving forward. If they can find it, they sometimes pull out a strategic plan. But the problem with many strategic planning documents is that there is not much strategy in them. They often look more like long-range operational plans.

Even if organizational leaders cannot articulate their organization's strategy, they usually have one. I call it the default strategy. It goes like this: "We are going to do the same thing we did last year in the same way, but we are going to try harder this time."

Almost every board can make a significant contribution to the organization by helping it to sharpen its strategy. Yet there is a lot of confusion about the board's role in strategy. Some organizational leaders desire the board's active involvement and others want them to stay out of it. The opinions are wide-ranging. For example:

- The board should actively create the overall strategy
- The board should be integrally involved in creating the strategy
- The board should have input at the beginning of the process
- The board should approve the strategy document
- The board should merely ensure the organization has a long-range plan

Who is responsible for developing the organizational strategy? Would it be wise for a board to dream up a new strategy and hand it down to the staff to execute? Some say that strategic planning is a management function so staff should do this work. If it is staff only, will the board be allowed to question the strategic plan? Is the board supposed to avoid thinking strategically in board meetings?

The process of developing a strategic plan may result in conflict between the board and staff or between board members. If the staff offers their best thinking, the board might criticize their plan. Several board members may offer their advice when they don't fully understand the external challenges and headwinds the organization is facing. Board members may sharply disagree among themselves about the direction the organization should go.

It might help if both board and staff understand the difference between a strategy and a strategic plan.

STRATEGIC PLANNING VS. STRATEGIC THINKING

A written strategic plan is static. Strategy is dynamic. Developing both requires strategic thinking.

Strategic thinking is focused on the relevant environment of the organization and how the organization is performing. It is less concerned about how things are done inside the black box and more concerned about the organization's match with the demands, challenges, and opportunities in its context.

Strategic planning that focuses on improving what is happening inside the black box tends to be minimally strategic. Strategy implies change. A strategic plan that aims to preserve the organization as is tends to be minimally strategic.

A typical strategic planning process has five parts. 1) It starts with a review and adjustments to foundational documents such as vision, mission statement, and core values. 2) Then some time is spent considering threats and opportunities outside of the organization. 3) The process identifies key result areas or critical success factors. 4) The process identifies goals and objectives for these key result areas. Arguments can ensue about which is over the other. Education majors tend to put goals higher than objectives and business majors tend to put objectives higher than goals. Sometimes these goals and objectives are set at an organization-wide level only and other times they are highly detailed and department specific. 5) The process often includes financial implications or budget projections to make it all happen. But where exactly do these strategic plans explain the strategy?

Any board and staff can keep things simple by acknowledging that a strategy is basically the path for moving forward. There is no need to make strategy overly complicated. The mission is what you do. The values are who you are. The vision is where you want to go. The strategy is how you will get from here to there.

Board members need to think strategically when they meet, but they do not have to do the strategic planning. Board members can contribute to the organization by engaging with strategy formation, but they do not have to write the strategic plan or even approve it. On the other hand, some boards will want to set the annual goals together with the organizational leader. It depends on what kind of board the organization has and the capabilities of the staff. No matter at what level or how detailed, it all involves strategic thinking.

Does any nonprofit organization really want a nonstrategic board?

STRATEGY AND ORGANIZATIONAL LIFECYCLE

All nonprofits are currently located somewhere on the organizational lifecycle. Like humans, organizations are born, grow, mature, age, and die. Unlike humans, organizations can reinvent themselves and move to a new growth phase through innovation, effectively starting a new lifecycle. Each phase of the lifecycle will require a different strategy for moving forward.

First, there is the startup phase where everything is exciting and new. Next, comes the growth phase where everything is up and to the right. But nothing grows forever, so all growing organizations hit plateaus. Some organizations find a way to get growing again. Some remain on the plateau for years. Many eventually lose momentum and enter the decline phase, which can last for decades. Some organizations find a way to make hard choices that return the organization to a season of growth. Those that can't adjust to a shifting environment eventually run out of cash and move into the terminal phase.

Each phase in the organizational lifecycle requires a different type of strategy.

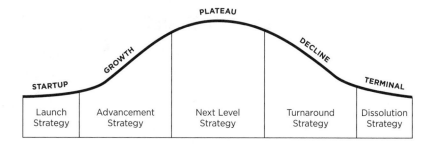

1. LAUNCH STRATEGY

Organizations in startup mode need a strategy built on experiments and "fast failures" with rapid iterations. They need to remain flexible and alert to opportunities as they arise. Typically, they will have a compelling vision and goals that are relatively short-term. Because they are starting something new, they will need to learn their way forward. If they do write a formal strategic plan, it will tend to grow stale quickly as events unfold.

2. ADVANCEMENT STRATEGY

For growing organizations, a strategy with longer-range goals is appropriate. Advancement strategies are about setting clear priorities and building capacity to handle growth. Capacity-building areas include office space, support staff, back office services, and growing the donor base. Because growth is happening naturally, there is little need to push the organization to move ahead. Instead, the organizational leaders need to remove obstacles and set clear priorities and growth targets. A formal, long-range strategic plan can be useful for strategic alignment throughout the organization.

3. NEXT LEVEL STRATEGY

For organizations on a plateau, growth has stalled. They are not in noticeable decline, but what used to be effective doesn't work as well anymore. It feels like they must push harder now to get the same results. They need a breakthrough. They want to take the organization to the next level, but they don't know how to get there. If this is the case, then they need a next level strategy.

They can find a new way forward by refining their ministry model, expanding to new groups to serve, adding new services, or starting a new division. On a plateau, organizations still have time to experiment and innovate. A formal, long range plan is helpful for managing current work, but the organization needs a breakthrough to get to the next level. This requires innovation.

This kind of strategy may involve forming a separate group to figure out a different way of working. Often, staff will resist making the kind of changes in the structure and methods required. A separate group can experiment with new methods with minimal interference from entrenched staff. For example, many colleges and universities faced so much resistance from faculty that they were forced to create separate divisions to develop and implement online learning.

4. TURNAROUND STRATEGY

Organizations riding the downhill side of the organizational lifecycle need a turnaround strategy. They must reinvent their way of working and their organization. Often, there is a general sense of dissatisfaction with organizational results. First, the leaders need to admit that the organization is in decline and not on a plateau. Some cost-cutting and right-sizing might be in order. A turnaround strategy deals with the root causes of the decline, ensures the right people are on the bus, and maps out a path for significant organizational change. Formal, long-range plans tend to be unhelpful because what the organization is currently doing isn't working. Instead, they need a short-term plan for an organizational make-over. If successful, the organization can complete the turnaround and move to a new growth curve.

All too often, board members want to respond to organizational decline by setting aggressive growth targets. But the organization is in decline for a reason. Sometimes it is because their ministry model or service they provide is no longer working as well as it used to. Something in the needs of the clients or the relevant environment has changed over time and demand or effectiveness has declined. Pouring gas on it will merely produce more lackluster results. First, the board and staff must figure out what has shifted. They need to find a new ministry model or delivery system or target audience. Once the organization has found a new way forward, then they can complete the turnaround and get on a fresh growth curve.

5. DISSOLUTION STRATEGY

Organizations that can't find the will to change or don't adapt to a changing context, will one day run out of cash and close. When entering the terminal phase, the organization needs a dissolution strategy. This plan is about shutting down with integrity, paying all bills, and selling or donating any remaining assets. It can take the form of merging with another nonprofit or selling property to developers. This plan needs to focus on the good stewardship of existing assets and shutting down with integrity.

Too many organizations wait until they get to a point of desperation before considering the possibility of a merger. If they wait too long, the organization may have little value left to offer. In fact, most nonprofit mergers turn out to be an acquisition. The weaker organization is absorbed by the healthier one. Exceptional boards tend to have an exit plan describing when, how, and why they might merge or close their organization way before they need to have one.

The board can certainly make a significant contribution by identifying where their nonprofit is sitting on the organizational lifecycle and assuring the proposed strategy is appropriate.

DELIBERATE STRATEGY VS. EMERGENT STRATEGY

Staff and boards sometimes experience conflict over whether to act in accordance with the written, approved, strategic plan or vary off it. Strategic plans need to be clear and communicated throughout the organization, but they also need to be flexible. Organizational leaders need to balance the use of both deliberate strategy and emergent strategy.

Deliberate strategy is the process of bringing a group together to analyze the organization and its context, describe a preferred future, set long-range and annual goals, then focus on execution of the plan. At some point, usually once a year for most nonprofits, organizational leaders bring the group together again to repeat the process. It relies on an objectives-oriented style of planning.

Emergent strategy is the process of bringing people together quarterly or annually to review what is working and what is not. It is about trying experiments, learning from them, and adjusting the strategy to what is working. It relies on a domain and direction style of planning.

Both are useful. One emphasizes organizational control and the other emphasizes organizational learning.

While written strategic plans keep the board, organizational leader, and staff all pointed in the same direction, all long-range, strategic plans are based on flawed assumptions about the future. Those involved in planning assume existing trends will continue, the organization will remain stable, the economy will experience no significant shocks, and there will be no "black swan" events. The relevant environment is always shifting, but quite slowly for some nonprofits, so slowly that they can easily miss it.

Organizations need to think strategically, make strategic plans, and periodically review their plans to incorporate what they are learning. They need to remain vigilant for new opportunities as they appear. As Peter Drucker said, opportunity only knocks once. More than ever, nonprofits today need a clear strategy, adaptive leaders, and flexible plans.

ELEMENTS OF STRATEGY

Written, strategic plans can be quite elaborate. They could include goals and objectives for one, three, and five years out. They could have goals and objectives specified down to the department level. But if the core of their strategy is off target, then many of their detailed goals and objectives will be off target. Their long list of objectives will spawn a bunch of disconnected projects and actions.

The core of any strategy or strategic plan should fit on one side of one sheet of paper. Richard Rumelt has proposed such an approach that he calls the "strategy kernel." The kernel, or fundamental core of a strategy, has three parts: diagnosis, guiding policy, and set of coherent actions.

Diagnosis: This is a high-level analysis of the organization describing what is going on internally and externally. What kind of situation are they facing? What is changing in the relevant environment? The purpose of this part is to provide significant insight. Using systems thinking tools can be useful here. It will often result in a list of key challenges.

Guiding policy: This is the strategic theme or the general strategic approach the organization will take. This is the most difficult of the three parts to grasp. I sometimes explain it as the guiding idea or strategic direction. It sums up the overall approach to overcoming the challenges the organization is facing but stops short of specifying how this will be accomplished.

Set of coherent actions: Once the guiding policy is clear, it must be implemented. Planners need to make a list of the key initiatives or projects for moving forward. This list should be high level and the actions clearly connected in a way that will produce impact. Every project does not need to be listed and no initiative needs to be described in detail at this point.

So, the set of coherent actions implement the guiding policy in order to overcome the challenges the organization is facing.

Once the strategy kernel is complete, it can be handed off to the management team and then departmental leaders for more detailed planning. If the strategy kernel is on track, then all the rest of the planning that takes place will be strategic. If the strategy kernel is clear, any organizational leader will be able to articulate the organization's strategy.

For example, I worked with the board of a nonprofit in a small city in the south that provided overnight shelter and counseling to homeless families. The founder of their 25-year-old ministry had retired and their new director was a former HR professional. The board decided they wanted some assistance with strategic planning because everybody recognized major changes were in order.

The challenges felt overwhelming when we finished listing them on the flip chart. The list included challenges such as:

- Stabilizing funding
- Upgrading technology
- Addressing mental illness and substance abuse
- Improving intake procedures
- Recruiting volunteers
- Enhancing the organizational image in the community
- Improving relationship with the city
- Remodeling the facility

Guiding policy, or guiding idea, is sometimes a full sentence and sometimes a poignant phrase. In this case, after a long discussion, the board captured the guiding policy in one word: Professionalize.

As soon as this became clear, they had a new vantage point and realized that the board had been overseeing a "mom and pop" organization. They needed to take the organization to the next level of efficiency and effectiveness.

This led to a clear set of coherent actions that built on each other.

- Improve fundraising hardware, software, and processes
- Improve administrative hardware, software, and processes
- Improve case management hardware, software, and processes
- Establish donor database with segmented lists
- Sharpen the mission statement and branding
- Remodel interior for enhanced functioning and privacy for guests

This list of coherent actions represented two or three years of work for this small, mostly volunteer organization.

How involved should a board become in developing the strategy kernel? Some will want to be integrally involved in the process, some will want the opportunity to give input up front and feedback towards the end, and some will want to delegate this process to the organizational leader and staff. Most of the planning that becomes more detailed, such as annual goals and departmental planning, should be delegated to the staff. A general principle as you go deeper in any organization is that the planners and the doers should be the same people.

STRATEGY CAN BE ELUSIVE

Sometimes, no matter what size the nonprofit organization, strategy can be obvious. For example, the board of a floundering nonprofit with an organizational leader who coasted during his last few years, needs a strategy to recruit a new organizational leader, overhaul the fundraising system, and figure out what new programs or services they might be able to provide to their community. They also might see the need to upgrade the board to policy-based governance. Together with the organizational leader, they can clearly see the "big rocks" and know what to do.

Other times, strategy can be elusive. I often draw organizational challenges as a mountain range. In terms of strategic direction, the organization can find a pass to climb over the mountains, drill a tunnel through to the other side, or turn around and head in a new direction. There is no template or tool to tell a board which option is best.

If comparing this to crossing a river with no bridge, the organization can build a raft and float across, drive to a bridge a few miles away, hire a plane to fly over, swim across, or stay on this side of the river. In general, any group should brainstorm many possible strategic directions and discuss them thoroughly to find the best alternative.

Sometimes, strategic options are difficult to generate. Here are a few case studies illustrating that the path forward is not always obvious for a board.

Agape Adoption Agency: A small social service agency has specialized in arranging for international adoptions between the US and Latin American countries. Due to new international law and recent changes in other nation's laws, international adoptions have plummeted by 90%. All but one of the nations they work with have temporarily banned any of their children from leaving the country. What should they do: Double down on international adoptions? Move into domestic adoptions? Cut expenses and wait it out? Become a social service agency serving families?

Camp Wannabe: A small, nondenominational camp offered summer camp programming for children and youth plus weekend retreats for congregations in their service area. The camp was able to fill only 60% of its beds last summer. Spending more money on marketing isn't working. Kids seem to be too busy with sports and other activities during the summer to go to camp. What should they do: Create new, exciting programming? Become a sports camp? Go through a rebranding exercise? Merge with a nearby "super camp"? Turn the camp into independent living for seniors? Sell the property to a developer and invest the assets in a related ministry?

Exhausted Association: This small, nonprofit organization was formed over fifty years ago to serve its members. They host an annual conference, publish a magazine, and offer other resource materials through their website. Increasingly, more of the members are asking what the organization has done for them lately. Membership has been in a steady decline. What should they do: Raise their rates? Organize regional gatherings? Deliver more services online? Merge with another association that has been a competitor?

Inspirational Publishing: This company grew quickly in the 1970s and 1980s by providing popular inductive Bible studies and Christian fiction. Throughout the demise of small Christian bookstores and then the collapse of retail chains, Inspirational Publishing tried to be upbeat. But sales were way down in their two top categories. Other big publishers got into the Christian fiction segment and captured all the best authors. Having always sold to bookstores, they do not know how to reach small group and Bible study leaders. What should they do: Build an email list to sell directly to small group leaders? Buy ads on Google and Facebook? Make all their inductive Bible studies available online at low cost? Help people self-publish their books?

Generic College: A small, private university has been struggling to recruit enough students each year and keep tuition at an affordable level. Today, parents are less likely to have put aside savings for a college fund for their children. Students are feeling more apprehensive about taking on the crushing burden of student loans. People are wondering if the education offered at a smaller school is worth it. What should they do: Dive into offering online degree programs? Partner with a marketing company to recruit more students? Cut costs to lower tuition to attract more students? Focus on majors that lead to high-paying jobs? Merge with another college?

Don't become discouraged if the strategy for your organization feels elusive. Here are options for getting organized.

ESTABLISHING A STRATEGY TEAM

Should the board be involved in strategy formation or just approve the strategic plan? There are three options for establishing a strategy team available to any organization: Board-led, Staff-led, and special task force.

Board-led: The board takes the lead in the strategy formation process by identifying the core strategy, together with the organizational leader, then handing this down to the staff to complete the planning process. Ideally, the board will secure input from the staff, if any, at the beginning of the process. They will also gather information about changes in the relevant environment. This option is common among smaller nonprofits or all-volunteer organizations.

Staff-led: The organizational leader takes the lead in the strategy formation process by identifying the core strategy, together with the staff, then bringing this to the board for approval before completing the rest of the planning process. Ideally, the organizational leader will secure input from the board at the beginning of the process. This is common with larger, more complex, nonprofit organizations.

Task force-led: The organizational leader assembles a special task force composed of some board members, some key staff, and perhaps some outside experts. This task force has no formal authority but is charged with integrating all perspectives and proposing a path for moving forward. The task force can solicit input from all sources and then seek feedback from staff and board to develop a final written document for board approval.

The question is not who should determine the organizational strategy. Nonprofits have three options for doing that work. The central point is that when the entire process is complete, whichever option is selected, both board and staff end up on the same page.

DECIDING ON A STRATEGY PROCESS

After the strategy team is decided, a process for strategy formation needs to be determined. This can be short and simple or longer and more complex, depending on the situation the organization is facing.

The first decision is determining the time horizon and boundaries for planning. Typical choices include one, three, five, and ten years out. Smaller organizations will lean toward a shorter time frame. Organizations of any size in a turbulent environment will lean toward a shorter time frame. More stable institutions will lean to a longer time frame. An organization can also set the time frame to coincide with a key event in the environment, like a governmental election. Boundaries include deciding how much data the organization will gather in the analysis phase and any issues that are nonnegotiable.

The second decision is determining the level of transparency that would be optimal with staff and other stakeholders. It can range from seeking input and feedback from a wide range of stakeholder groups to a closed process. If there are trust issues between the staff and board due to what has happened in the past, an organization may choose a more open process. If a nonprofit is working to avert bankruptcy and layoffs, they may choose a more closed process to reduce unnecessary panic.

The third decision is determining the number of steps to build into the process. These could include asking for staff input, asking for donor input, conducting an environmental scan, holding an analysis meeting, holding a draft strategy formation meeting, seeking feedback from the board, seeking feedback from the staff, holding a final strategy formation meeting, bringing the strategy document to the board for approval, then bringing the approved strategy to the staff to launch the more detailed levels of planning. An organization can choose a simple process to complete in one day or a more elaborate process requiring several meetings over several weeks.

For example, with a larger nonprofit organization on the east coast, the management team decided that a more elaborate process would be best for their situation. Because of trust issues between management and staff, they opted for starting with seeking input from the staff, all 300 of them. We decided that I would interview them in groups of 10-20 across their five service centers. We used a set of seven open-ended questions to elicit their opinions on what was going well, what needed to be improved, and what they thought the organization should do. In the end, over 50% of the employees participated in one of the groups. We then compiled all their responses verbatim, without any editing, and distributed them by email to all employees. Each person knew the information was unfiltered because they could see their response was captured accurately. This step alone increased both the level of employee trust and the feeling of urgency for change.

Then, they decided to conduct an in-depth environmental scan including what was changing in the local economy, state regulations, key societal trends, legalization of marijuana, and concerns of donors. We assigned each topic to a team of three, carefully selected staff people. Peer pressure kicked in a bit and the reports coming out of each team looked like something one would receive from a professional research firm.

Then we held the first meeting. The task force included the top management team plus a few key staff with special expertise. No board members were invited. We completed the analysis of what was happening in the relevant environment and within the organization. Then we drafted the challenges, guiding policy, and key initiatives.

This draft strategy was brought before the board for feedback. After a few small adjustments, it was circulated to all staff with an opportunity to give feedback directly to the organizational leader by email.

All the email responses were compiled and sent to the strategy team. Then we met a second time to refine the diagnosis, guiding policy, and key initiatives. This was brought to the board for final approval.

Then the core strategy was delivered to the staff to set annual goals and objectives at the organizational level and down to department level. A dashboard of the key initiatives was created to track progress on a quarterly basis and adjust the strategy as needed.

Here is what happens in those quarterly meetings.

CONDUCTING STRATEGIC REVIEWS

Any written, long-range plan will grow stale over time. Seasonal strategic reviews will keep them fresh and up to date. But the nature of a season will differ between nonprofit organizations.

Some nonprofits will benefit by conducting strategic reviews quarterly. This is because larger organizations tend to compile financial reports quarterly. For churches and other organizations, seasonal reviews generally mean three times a year: Spring, Summer, Fall. For schools, a season means planning for Fall semester and Spring semester. For many smaller nonprofits, season means an annual strategic planning meeting.

Generally, a strategic review is a meeting with no tactical items on the agenda. It could be board only, staff only, or a special task force. It will typically cover five questions:

1. What was supposed to happen?

2. What actually occurred?

3. What went well and why? What can be improved and how?

4. How do we need to adjust the strategy?

5. What must happen in this next time period?

These questions are adapted from the After Action Review process developed by the US military for organizational learning and continuous improvement. Any nonprofit can use this approach to keep organizational strategy fresh.

Managing, governing, and navigating boards can all be strategic, but usually in different ways.

MANAGING BOARDS AND STRATEGY

In terms of the black box, managing boards make the major decisions about what happens inside of the box as well as keeping an eye on what is happening in the relevant environment. A managing board can act on both the strategic and management levels but will tend to be distracted by the immediate concerns and issues in operations.

Managing boards will tend to initiate the strategic planning process rather than delegate it to staff. The board may engage the whole board in the process if they are smaller or appoint a committee to do this work if they are larger in number. A managing board may also want to be involved in setting the annual goals or objectives together with the organizational leader. Sometimes, the reason for this is that if the board did not set the annual goals, nobody would.

One potential trap is that the board will obsess on trying to fix the organization rather than realizing the relevant environment has shifted and major changes must occur, not minor adjustments. For example, failing programs might need to be discontinued due to lack of demand and new programs or services need to be created.

Another trap is that the board will focus on operations and fail to look outside the organization for input from current clients, past clients, donors, and other community leaders.

GOVERNING BOARDS AND STRATEGY

In terms of the black box, governing boards tend to oversee what is happening and focus on ends policies rather than strategy. They want to ensure the organization has a long-range strategic plan but may or may not ask to formally approve it. They may or may not want input into the strategy formation process. This may be because of the complexity of the work of the organization and their relative lack of expertise.

Organizational leaders may also ask the board to stay out of strategic planning and direct them to focus on ends policies. They may assert that strategic planning is dealing with means and therefore in the realm of the organizational leader, not the board. On the other hand, a board might agree to stay out of detailed strategic planning but want to be involved in the process of high-level strategy formation because it is so tightly connected to achieving the results of the organization.

A governing board can ask to be integrally involved in the strategy formation process or ask to approve the organizational strategy. In either case, their attention should be focused on making progress towards ends and not getting involved in operational planning processes.

NAVIGATING BOARDS AND STRATEGY

In terms of the black box, navigating boards will be ultra-concerned about shaping strategy. Whether a new start-up or an aging nonprofit, a navigating board will want to partner with the organizational leader to figure out how best to move forward.

An effective navigating board will tend to have board members who are more experienced in strategy or have more knowledge of the industry than the organizational leader. They may have experienced a merger or acquisition, or they may have had to make the tough calls in the past. Rather than giving advice, they are working together with the organizational leader as a team to find the best path forward.

Navigating boards will tend to spend less time dealing with routine agenda items and move quickly to the strategic questions at hand. They will be thinking more about where to move the box or reshape it rather than how to improve what is happening inside.

A trap for all navigating boards is to determine the strategy and then slide into managing the execution of the strategy, thereby functioning as a managing board. The secret for effectiveness of navigating boards is to keep the lid of the box shut and delegate all management to the organizational leader.

While all boards have the potential to make a significant contribution regarding strategy, they also have the potential to make a significant contribution in fundraising and developing new sources of income.

CHAPTER 9

THE BOARD'S ROLE
IN FUNDRAISING

No organizational leader ever wants to hear a new board member ask in a meeting, "You mean I'm supposed to help raise money?" Even if they don't verbalize it, a lot of new board members may experience a similar reaction. If assisting with fundraising is an expectation of each board member, then potential board members should be made aware of this while being recruited for service and before their first board meeting.

Sometimes the expectation is not made clear because there is a lot of confusion regarding how involved a board ought to be in fundraising. Some will say fundraising is the primary responsibility of the board, that the board's first job is to ensure adequate resources to operate. Others will say every board member should be making a significant financial donation. Still others firmly believe that fundraising is not something board members should be expected to do.

GOVERNANCE AND FUNDRAISING

Securing funding is certainly critical for any organization but it does not represent the work of governance. It is an activity, just like serving as a volunteer in the organization. Yet, boards are not prohibited from giving personally or helping to secure donations.

John Carver explained that, strictly speaking, fundraising is not a function of governance. Yet, if any board decides it wants to assist with fundraising, then it can make that an expectation for all board members and add it to the policy manual. Similarly, any board can set an expectation that all board members will serve as a regular, front-line volunteer. This could include such volunteer opportunities as tutoring for a literacy organization or cleaning cages at a pet rescue organization. While these duties are significant, they do not represent the important work of governance.

FUNDRAISING BOARDS

To add to the confusion, some groups unapologetically call themselves fundraising boards. This is especially true for new startups and small, all-volunteer organizations. Because the financial need is so great and the governance duties so quickly dealt with, most of their time and energy is directed at raising the necessary funds to operate and grow.

Established or historic institutions, like large universities or museums, may also spend more time and energy on building their endowment or participating in a capital campaign rather than governance work. They might only recruit individuals with major donor potential for their board or may require a sizeable donation before being accepted onto the board. They tend to function more like fundraising societies than governing boards. These boards may have an executive committee, or a governance committee, tasked with fulfilling most of the governance duties while they focus on fundraising.

In a time of crisis, any board may become consumed by the financial challenges and neglect their oversight of the rest of the organization. Their focus becomes finding new donors and new sources of income. While they would not call themselves a fundraising board, they would temporarily act like one.

In some cases, it might be cleaner to create a committee or separate auxiliary group to focus on the fundraising task. These can be affinity groups or branded societies such as "Friends of (the organization)" or the "Blue Ribbon Commission for (the cause)" or the "The (President's) Cabinet." Legally, they would be formed as committees of the board and under the authority of the board. They could also be organized as a separate foundation but dedicated to the same cause. These groups are then free to focus on the fundraising task without worrying about the governance duties. The organization can then recruit the most experienced people for the board and the most influential donors for their auxiliary group.

Organizational leaders and development directors are sometimes reluctant to form these separate auxiliary groups. They assume that those they want to recruit would like the prestige of being on the official board. But serving faithfully on a board can represent a lot of unwanted work for busy people. Plus, an affinity group such as a branded society can be made to be quite prestigious as well.

INFLUENCE AND AFFLUENCE

If a board determines that it wants all board members to be involved in fundraising for the organization, then it can set clear expectations for individual board members in three areas. Board members have a lot to offer through influence as well as affluence. It does not matter whether the board is a managing, governing, or a navigating type of board. All board members can be asked to donate, communicate, and collaborate.

Donate: The board can set an expectation that all board members give financially to the organization. If a nonprofit is a charitable organization that solicits donations from others, then it can be a severe negative if some of the board members do not donate to the organization they oversee. The expectation for donation level can be expressed as a minimum dollar amount per year. Without being legalistic, it can be expressed as board members being "active donor" or "generous giver" or "donor of record" of the organization.

For some organizations, the organizational leader or development director will sit down with each board member individually to discuss their annual giving. With other organizations, the board chair may choose to have an open discussion with the board and ask for all gifts to be contributed by a certain date.

By giving individually, board members lead by example. This also gives them added courage to make a contribution in two other ways.

Communicate: The board can set an expectation that board members speak out for the cause or the organization in various ways. This can be done in person or using their preferred social media channels. They can ask people to pray, volunteer, sign up for a newsletter, or attend a special event.

In addition to opportunities that occur in normal conversation, they can volunteer to give presentations to other groups or meet individually with community leaders to share stories about what the organization has accomplished.

Collaborate: The board can set an expectation that board members will work together with the organizational leader or development department to tap their contact list. Board members can share names of prospective donors or sponsors for special events.

These connections can be made by setting up personal appointments, sending an email message introducing the prospect and staff person, or simply sharing names and contact information for the development director to follow up.

Board members can also participate in the donor cultivation process. About 90% of the development process is cultivation. They can invite prospective donors to special events and join in on appointments with the development staff. Only 10% of the development process is about making the ask for money.

DON'T MAKE THE ASK

The biggest fear of board members in assisting with fundraising is asking for a donation. The simplest solution is to tell them board members don't need to make the ask.

Most board members are untrained volunteers when it comes to asking major donors for gifts. They will tend to choke during the conversation. So, let them off the hook.

Board members can offer names of prospects, they can set up appointments, they can be at the meeting and share their passion for the organization, but in most cases, they should not make the ask. Board members should not decide how much a prospective major donor should give, they will usually underestimate. Leave it to the pros.

This should bring considerable relief to board members who are uncomfortable asking for money and make them more willing to donate, communicate, and collaborate with the organizational leader or development director.

CULTURE OF GENEROSITY

A key for getting the board more involved in development and for securing more donations is to build a culture of generosity throughout the entire organization: Board, staff, clients, and donors. Infuse the entire organization with a spirit of giving. Boards should not treat fundraising like a necessary evil.

Ideally, most organizations would want an organizational culture marked by gratitude instead of greediness. This can be done by sharing stories of changed lives and bringing people together around shared values. Organizations need simple ways or clear on-ramps to bring in new donors and volunteers.

If a board has a fundraising committee, its purpose should not be to do all the work, but to help every board member understand how they can donate, communicate, and collaborate.

FUNDRAISING MIX

Boards can make a significant contribution by examining the current mix of fundraising tactics. Some organizations rely heavily on direct mail, some on special events, and others on major donor cultivation. There are about a dozen different categories of fundraising tactics. Every organization needs to figure out its own optimum mix.

Too many organizations have been doing the same thing the same way for years. Others have been adding new tactics because they heard it worked well for someone else. Boards can ask productive questions about funding sources and methods that can help the organization fine-tune its mix.

All charitable nonprofits need to define a pathway for donors, the different levels on that pathway, and the tactics they will use to move them from one level to the next. For example, the levels could look like this:

Friend/Prospect → Initial gift/Contact information → Second gift → Occasional donor → Regular donor → Major donor

The tactics that help move outsiders to make an initial gift will not work as well to help regular donors make a major gift. Every organization needs to design what works for them.

The tactics that are right for one organization may not work for another. For example, grant writing and planned giving may be out of reach for many organizations.

Following are categories of fundraising tactics any organization can draw upon.

Digital: This is a fast-changing category that includes sending email to segmented lists, having a website, and being active on social media. It includes buying Facebook or Google ads, buying banner ads on websites, and using text messaging to give small amounts immediately or sign up for a mailing list. It includes apps dedicated to crowdfunding. Digital tactics tend to be more effective in securing new donors and smaller gifts. Using Twitter will not make a nonprofit suddenly sustainable.

In-kind gifts: This category is about asking individuals or businesses for donations of products or services. These gifts can be intended for office use such as used desks and chairs, for special events like a silent auction, or for clients such as baby blankets and disposable diapers. Some in-kind gifts, like used automobiles, can be converted to cash.

Annual drive: This category is an annual event or campaign intended to cover basic operating expenses of an organization or program. A school might have an annual drive in the Fall to cover the cost of audio-visual equipment and educational supplies. An organization may have an annual phone-a-thon to raise money and new donors. Giving Tuesday has recently emerged as a way many organizations can promote an annual drive simultaneously following Black Friday, Small Business Saturday, and Cyber Monday.

Special events: This category tends to be more time-intensive for staff and volunteers and includes banquets, house parties, walk-a-thons, bike rides, golf tournaments, silent auctions, car washes (or even bar crawls). Events can be used effectively for engaging friends of the organization, securing new donors, and raising money. When an event becomes less effective over time or even loses money, it may be time to switch to another kind of event or to another fundraising tactic.

Sustaining donors: This category includes donors who are committed to giving regularly, whether monthly or annually. Examples include sponsoring a child in another country or supporting a missionary. The organization keeps in touch with the donor through a monthly letter or email message. Gifts are sent by check through the mail or by automatic deduction.

Major donors: This category includes gifts over a certain dollar amount. The financial threshold varies widely between nonprofits. Larger nonprofits will tend to have segmented their major donors into several levels, for example, major donors and mega donors.

Working with major donors is 90% cultivation and 10% activation. Organizations may create branded societies or hold retreats exclusively for people in this category.

Grants: This category includes gifts from foundations, corporations, and government sources. Securing grants tends to be a highly bureaucratic process requiring the hiring of a professional grant writer. Many grantors will ask for extensive documentation of program plans and evidence of past outcomes.

Planned gifts: This category includes all aspects of estate planning including wills, charitable remainder trusts, annuities, life insurance, and donor-advised funds. Assisting the donor will usually require the services of a lawyer or financial planner. Large, more stable institutional nonprofits tend to benefit from these tactics than smaller, community-based organizations.

Capital campaigns: This category includes coordinated efforts to raise large amounts of money in a specific amount of time to build a or remodel a facility, create an endowment, or retire debt. Usually, these are planned around a 3-5-year period. Donors are asked to commit to give a certain amount within that time frame. Many nonprofits will benefit from hiring an outside consultant to manage the campaign. This kind of tactic should not be undertaken lightly.

Boards can make a significant contribution to their organization by asking questions about the current mix of fundraising tactics and the ideal mix. Every organization needs to design its unique mix of tactics and keep reviewing it to keep it fresh and effective.

Common mistakes nonprofits make include over-reliance on direct mail, no major donor plan, lack of new donor acquisition plan, and hoping for the miracle gift to come along. How a board goes about taking action to find the right mix of tactics depends on what type of board they are.

MANAGING BOARDS

Regarding fundraising, this type of board tends to open the lid of the black box and examine income and expenses. If out of balance, they will tend to look for ways to cut expenses first, then look at ways to increase income later.

In a crisis, members of these boards will tend to suggest ideas for a new event and sometimes volunteer to coordinate the event. This could be done by forming a committee or by serving as volunteers to the organizational leader. They will also tend to assist with existing events or fundraising efforts.

Expectations about what board members should do regarding fundraising should be made clear in the board member job description.

GOVERNING BOARDS

Regarding fundraising, this type of board tends to look at resources going into the black box and results coming out the other side. While trying to stay out of operations and avoiding micromanagement, board members will tend to ask questions about funding sources and the mix of fundraising tactics.

In a crisis, members of these boards will tend to encourage and support the organizational leader and offer to assist by calling or meeting with existing donors and by providing leads to potential new donors. They may sharpen their statements regarding cost in their ends policies regarding sources of funding. In limitations policies, they may restrict certain kinds of fundraising efforts that might damage organizational branding or put the organization at risk in some other way. For example, they may prohibit bike-a-thons, car washes, renting mailing lists, or selling pizza kits or any other food items. If board members are local, they may also volunteer to assist with special events.

Expectations for board members regarding fundraising efforts should be included in the governance process section of their board policy manual.

NAVIGATING BOARDS

Regarding fundraising, this type of board will be less concerned about what is happening inside the black box and more concerned about reconfiguring the whole system to make it easier to fund. They will tend to examine funding sources over time, note what is changing, and compare the mix of fundraising tactics to the relevant environment. For example, perhaps using direct mail to offer a Christmas ornament as an incentive for new donors used to work years ago, but it no longer does. Perhaps the annual Autumn banquet was a sure winner in the past, but now it loses money.

Navigating boards will watch for any new sources of funding or new methods of fundraising that may appear. They will pay attention to changing conditions and watch for new opportunities. For example, they might recommend new ideas for earned revenue which have not been explored in the past.

In a crisis, this type of board will tend to cut what is not working and look for new fundraising tactics that match the current context. They will be quick to abandon unproductive events. They will tend to look at other similar organizations to see what they are doing. They may ask the organizational leader to run several experiments to see what works.

Expectations for these board members regarding fundraising don't need to be spelled out. They will instinctively work to make the changes in the fundraising system for sustainable mission fulfillment. For example, they might work to establish multiple streams of revenue, introduce or raise fees for services provided, or seek one-time grants for organizational transformation.

In summary, fundraising is not technically a function of governance. Yet, board members who are passionate about the organization they oversee will naturally want to give personally, tell others about the organization, and assist the staff with fundraising efforts. Effective boards will decide how involved its members will be in the task of fundraising and make these expectations clear in the job description or in the board policy manual.

Sometimes, dysfunctional behavior makes it difficult for a board to make a significant contribution. If a board has a problem, then the board should deal with it.

CHAPTER 10

BOARD BREAKDOWNS

A few years ago, I was hired to assist a board of a large nonprofit organization solve some of the issues it was having. While doing my homework before the meeting, I asked the organizational leader for a copy of their board policy manual and scheduled some phone calls with board members. Their board policy manual was well-written, and I surmised that they had hired an outside consultant to help them develop it. While interviewing the long-time board chair over the telephone, I asked her if the board was policy-based. She said yes. I asked her how it was working, and she said very well. While holding the document in my hand, I asked her if they had written policies compiled in a board policy manual. She said she didn't think so.

Even with solid training and the right tools in place, board performance can deteriorate over time. Here is what researchers and scholars have said about the overall performance of boards:

"There is one thing all boards have in common . . . they do not function."—Peter Drucker

"Trustees are little more than high-powered, well-intentioned people engaged in low-level activities." —Richard Chait, Thomas Holland, Barbara Taylor

"Boards have been largely irrelevant throughout most of the twentieth century." —James Gillies

"Ninety-five percent of boards are not fully doing what they are legally, morally and ethically supposed to do." —Harold Geneen

"Boards tend to be, in fact, incompetent groups of competent individuals." —John Carver

All boards have problems from time to time. But effective boards work on their problems and strive to make a significant contribution as a group. Those who do not address their problems can become dysfunctional and make things worse for their organization instead of better. Following are common problems or issues boards face grouped into nine general areas. These are all causes of board ineffectiveness.

BOARD STRUCTURE

This area includes all aspects of how a board is formed, when and where they meet, and how it relates to operations. This is usually prescribed in the organization's bylaws and board process policies.

Board is too large: Some organizations have over 50 people serving on their board. At some point in the history of each of these organizations, somebody thought the board needed to add more members. The reasons for this vary. It could have been for broader representation. It could have been a result of inviting potential major donors on the board. But large boards tend to make governance less effective because it makes intelligent conversation and group decision-making more difficult.

As a workaround, many organizations form committees with an executive committee determining which issues are handled by them and which go to the full board. But this structure can unintentionally make people feel like the executive committee is flying in business class while the rest of the board is back in the economy section.

Some form a governance committee to care for board policies and recruit new board members. But these committees often fall into microgoverning mode or allow the full board to move into status quo governance mode. Other committees, such as HR, tend to get too involved in management issues.

One solution is to change the bylaws to reduce the number of members on the board. This can be done through attrition as board members term out, or by asking several board members to resign.

For those institutions that use board membership as a cultivation tool for major donors, they might do better by creating a separate, affinity group or branded society that more effectively cultivates potential donors.

Board bounces back and forth between governing and managing: This is a common problem for governing boards. It is difficult for many individuals to stick with overseeing the organization and stay out of management.

Board members who are passionate about the organization want to help, and they often give advice regarding operational matters. Some board members are gifted at management, and they want to use their strengths on the board. When they hear about a problem in the organization, they want to drill down, get to root causes, and offer a fix. Other board members feel a need to "check in" with staff before a board meeting and investigate any complaints the staff may have.

It often takes peer pressure from other board members to keep these people out of management issues.

Developing written policies and actively using them can help a governing board stick to governing. The board should also be able to clearly articulate what is board work and what is staff work. There is a fine line between monitoring and meddling. The general principle is for board members to "keep their nose in and their hands out."

Still, it is easy for many board members to jump into operational matters. Any board member should feel free to call a time out and ask if they are currently doing board work or staff work. The black box metaphor is useful for helping board members stick to a governing posture as well.

Tension between the organizational leader and board chair: Sometimes a new board chair gets elected who does not get along well with the organizational leader. Or perhaps a new board chair does not like the direction the organization is heading and wants to steer it a different way. Open conflict between the organizational leader and board chair during a board meeting is clearly dysfunctional.

This can be dealt with by having the board chair and organizational leader talk ahead of time and build the agenda for the board meeting together. This allows them to preview the discussion items, so they are on the same page and neither is caught off guard in the meeting.

If the ongoing conflict cannot be resolved, the rest of the board should move to appoint a new board chair if the bylaws and board policies permit it.

Executive committee usurps authority: This can be intentional or unintentional. With an executive committee of the board, usually there is a lack of clarity regarding which issues will be decided by the committee and which should be brought to the entire board. For example, if a bid for routine building maintenance is quite expensive, should the executive committee approve it or bring it to the entire board for a vote?

To resolve this, the board should write up clear guidelines or a board policy describing which decisions are made by the executive committee and which are made by the full board. Some organizations retain the executive committee but ask them to meet only during emergencies when the full board is unable to gather. This can be useful for national organizations that can appoint local board members to serve in this capacity.

BOARD MEMBERS

This area includes who is selected to serve on the board, how they behave, and how they work together as a team.

Board members arrive unprepared: Those selected for board service, or elected to the position, tend to be busy people. So, sometimes they struggle to review board materials sent ahead of time. Boards work best when all members arrive fully prepared.

Expectations are key, so make sure board members know they are to prepare thoroughly for all board meetings. As much as possible, send all materials ahead of time by mail or email. The board as a group should decide how many days in advance that they prefer to receive this information. They should also specify what kind of reports they want and at what level of detail.

Board members are disengaged: Some board members may tire of being on the board, lose passion for the work, or fail to attend board meetings. Expectations should be clear that if any board member is ill, out of town, or otherwise not able to attend a board meeting, that board member should email, text, or call the board chair ahead of time. A board can also add a written policy or guideline that if any member has two unexcused absences during a term, he or she is automatically removed from the board.

Board engagement can be enhanced by making sure the organization is recruiting high-quality board members and taking the necessary time to help them build strong relationships with each other. It can also be enhanced by working together on real challenges the organization is facing or may face soon.

Board members don't want to learn: Sometimes people serving on governing boards don't want to read about how policy-based governance works. Sometimes people on managing boards don't want to learn about what is changing for other organizations like theirs. Even if the organizational leader buys a book for everybody, they might not read it.

Again, expectations are key. Board members should be committed to continuous improvement throughout the organization, including its own governance practices. Policy-based governance has a steep learning curve for new board members. In order to be the best board that they can be for the organization, all board members need to be open to learning and growing in their position.

Board members lack key knowledge or skills: Rarely does a board have all the expertise it needs within itself to oversee the organization and chart a course for success. Navigating boards will tend to feel the greatest need for new information and expertise as they prepare to make major changes and venture out into new areas.

Some boards can recruit new board members whenever needed to gain this expertise. If the bylaws will not allow that, then they can form new committees and recruit outside people to serve a temporary role to supply what they need. They can also invite guest presenters to a board meeting including clients, funders, or community leaders. Boards can also hire a consultant or coach to serve as a guide during unusual times.

Board members don't speak up: Especially in larger boards, some board members will go through entire meetings without contributing any thoughts to the conversation. Obviously, they cannot make a significant contribution if they don't speak up.

Boards need to hear from everybody, not just the vocal few. A good board chair will take time to go around the room and make sure everybody has a chance to weigh in on important discussions. The board chair can also ask specific questions to individuals who may have useful information or opinions. He or she may also bring in a skilled facilitator for critical discussions when everybody needs to participate, including the board chair.

Board member is divisive: Boards work best when they are working together as a high-performing team. Yet some people tend to be highly political and love to pit "us" against "them." They call individual board members between meetings to win them over to their side. In general, no board member should be representing any single constituency or position, but all board members should adopt the perspective that they represent all stakeholders and the entire organization. This leaves less room for divisiveness to fester. All board members should strive to be good team players.

Board member is behaving badly: Bad behavior can exhibit itself in many forms. For example, using demeaning language, humiliating other board members, yelling, pounding on the table, swearing indignantly, or standing on a chair and calling other board members stupid. This kind of behavior persists because it is condoned by the rest of the board.

No board member needs to tolerate this kind of verbal abuse. When it occurs, the board chair should halt the meeting and deal directly with the offensive behavior. If this does not happen, the board chair should meet with the offending person one-to-one or with a few other board members. If that does not correct the problem, then the entire board should discuss the unacceptable behavior at the beginning of its next board meeting. If that is not enough, then the board should follow its bylaws or board policies to remove the offending person from the board.

Attempting to appease angry board members only rewards them for their bad behavior. Few boards can be truly effective with one or more board members who are behaving badly. Good board chairs will put a stop to it.

BOARD MEETINGS

This area includes typical agendas for board meetings, how long meetings last, who is invited in, and how the board chair facilitates the meetings.

Board meetings usually go late: it is not unusual for evening board meetings of nonprofits to go late into the night. This is due to several factors, including long agendas, lack of preparation of board members, and board members delving into micromanaging. The board chair should be the person who manages the discussion and determines when some items should be pushed forward to the next meeting.

It is possible to end meetings on time with a simple board policy that says something such as all board meetings will start at 7:00 and end promptly at 9:00, unless the board decides by unanimous vote to extend the meeting. Managing boards may also set a similar guideline and include it in their operations handbook.

A firm start and stopping time will put pressure on the board chair to plan the agenda well and put the most pressing topics early in the meeting. It will also help board members know when any topic has been discussed thoroughly enough.

Board chair facilitates poorly: Sometimes board members don't listen well and over talk each other frequently. This does not lead to high-quality conversation. One of the roles of the board chair is to facilitate the conversations and manage the agenda so each item receives enough attention. But what if the board chair is weak in this area?

One solution is to have the board chair appoint another board member with these skills to lead the meetings. The board chair is still in authority, but this allows him or her to participate in the discussion without worrying about facilitating it.

Reports are too detailed: Sometimes financial reports can be twenty pages long and staff activity reports can go on and on. In general, the board should decide what reports it wants to receive and what level of detail the reports will contain. Reports to the board should not be staff driven. In practice they often are because the staff is operating in a vacuum. Most boards don't take the time to specify what reports they want to receive.

For governing boards, too much reporting is about what is happening in the black box. While the board should be aware of how the organization is doing, it would be better for them to ask for reports about resources going into the box and results coming out the other side. Managing boards need more detail about what is happening inside the box, but they will want more high-level reporting and avoid asking too many questions about operational details. The board can ask for exception reporting from the organizational leader, so they are only informed about any irregularities occurring in operations.

Board gets dragged into micromanaging: Governing boards need to discipline themselves to stay out of operations. Managing boards need to discipline themselves to function at the executive level when they meet. But anyone can derail an otherwise effective board by asking seemingly innocent questions. For example, someone may ask what brand of photocopy machine the staff is going to buy and what features it will have.

Boards also get dragged into the weeds by an organizational leader who may want some input on a decision he or she needs to make. Many boards will respond by asking for more information, usually about operational details. Then they will debate the pros and cons of each option. While it might lead to an interesting discussion, it is not governing, and it is not making important decisions. It is merely giving advice on low level decisions.

Board wants additional staff in meetings: Some boards will want additional staff in the board meeting in case they have a question. Additional staff beyond the organizational leader makes it more difficult for the board to speak openly about organizational performance. It also blurs the single point of accountability a governing board usually wants with the organizational leader.

A managing board may want additional staff in the meetings to more efficiently work together with the leadership. A governing board will want to avoid bringing in other staff because it will pull them into management discussions and decisions. If they do, they will schedule staff reports at the beginning of the meeting and excuse them when they are done. A navigating board may want other outside experts invited to meetings to gather expert opinions or to help them learn about changes in the relevant environment. Existing staff will tend to resist the kind of changes a navigating board is contemplating.

Board keeps giving advice: In the spirit of being helpful, board members often offer advice to the organizational leader regarding operational details, solving a problem, or making a decision. But if a board offers advice, can an organizational leader ignore the advice?

For a governing board that wants to delegate management of the organization, advice giving regarding operations is out of bounds. For a managing board that wants to operate at a high level, they either make the decision or delegate it. They also want to stay out of the weeds. In general, advice giving is a total waste of breath if the organizational leader is not asking for advice.

Board has parking lot meetings: These are unofficial meetings where some of the board members feel a need to gather before or after the board meeting. These unofficial meetings can be reduced by holding executive sessions either at the beginning or end of each board meeting. An executive session is a short period of time when the organizational leader and any other staff are excused, and the board members can ask questions and sort out any concerns they may have.

Board members violating confidentiality: For most nonprofit organizations, board deliberations need to be held in confidence. In general, board minutes should report board actions, but not all the conversation leading up to the action. Specifically, the minutes should not state who or how many board members were holding what opinion. The minutes do not have to share what the vote was on any topic either, just that the board decided.

If confidential details of board deliberations are leaking out, the board chair should remind board members to hold board conversations in confidence. Each year, all board members should sign a confidentiality agreement and a conflict of interest statement. Doing this regularly prevents the need to bring out the forms when rumors start flying.

BOARD POLICIES

This area includes the four sections of governing policies captured in the board policy manual for a governing board as well as operating procedures captured in the organizational handbook for a managing board.

Board policies difficult to use: Board policy manuals can become a complicated mess over time. Sometimes the policy indents can go five or six levels deep. Many of the more detailed points are written in phrases, not complete sentences. Some policies are just a long list of detailed limitations.

This happens because the board has not been using a disciplined approach of nested sets, beginning with the broadest policies first, then moving down one level as a time as needed without skipping levels. Well-written policies at the higher level can eliminate the need for more detailed lists.

As new policies are added, they should be placed in the appropriate category and not simply tacked on to the end of a section. Sometimes an entire rewrite is required to make the policy manual easier to use.

Board manual too long: In an attempt to be thorough, some boards write board policy manuals that near a hundred pages in length. This is because they are adding other sections to store other foundational documents, such as the mission statement or core values statement. While these documents are important, they are not governing policies. Many of these are management tools that should be stored in a different place.

Boards with several permanent committees may want to add the policies they have developed for their committee work. In this case, they can be placed in an appendix to reduce the clutter in the main board policy manual.

Board policies overly detailed: Some boards write limitations policies that go into way too much detail. This is especially common for the section about financial matters. If a board is worried about something that might not be handled correctly, they will want to keep getting more and more specific about what is not allowed. This sometimes is driven by a governing board that is trying to manage the organization through limitations policies.

Some governing boards grow frustrated stating all the limitations policies in the negative, that is, what the organizational leader and staff may not do. So, they rewrite them all in positive form specifying how things are to be done in the organization. This small change essentially flips them over to serving as a managing board. If the organization is in decline, this transition may be just what is needed. Where it makes sense, these policies, written in positive or directive form, should be considered part of the organizational handbook.

Board does not use existing policies: Some boards claim to be governing boards but spend most of their time making decisions and advising the organizational leader. Their decisions are captured in the minutes instead of being translated into board policies. Some boards have a written policy manual and but never refer to it when meeting.

Before deciding on any issue, every governing board should first see if an existing policy covers the situation. If not, then they should write a policy to cover it. If the issue is an operational matter, the board may also hand the decision back to the organizational leader to make.

For example, a piece of equipment may need a costly repair that brings up the question of buying a new one rather than repairing it. The board may not have a policy about replacing equipment. This decision is clearly an operational matter, but one that would easily drag a governing board into management decisions. For a managing board, this is the kind of decision they are supposed to make. But a managing board may also delegate the decision back to the organizational leader.

FIDUCIARY RESPONSIBILITY

This area is a basic duty of all boards. A fiduciary is someone who accepts the responsibility of stewarding the property or assets of another. All board members serve as a fiduciary with the responsibility to care for the best interests of their nonprofit organization.

Board does not monitor financial condition: Some boards do not actively monitor the financial condition of the organization. This is one of their legal duties as a board. They should make sure all money is protected from fraud and is managed well. They should make sure the organization is financially stable.

This lack of attention can result from an organization having a large enough reserve in place or enough cash coming in that there is not much to worry about. But boards should ask for longer range financial forecasts and any assets that might be at risk.

A budget is a management tool. As such, a governing board will tend to overlook variances on the budget reports and focus on the bottom line and the bigger picture. A managing board will tend to review the regular budget reports in finer detail to assure that the organization stays out of financial trouble.

Board does not monitor income: While most boards will be concerned about the bottom line and a deficit in the budget, they will tend to give less attention to the income line. This is sometimes because they feel they have the power to cut expenses but feel less capable to increase donations.

Many smaller nonprofits in financial trouble do not have a budget problem. They have a fundraising problem. Whether the board is a governing or managing board, they should examine the mix of fundraising tactics and analyze what is changing.

Board members don't understand financial reports: Many board members do not have a degree in finance or extensive experience dealing with complicated budgets. Yet, the entire board should fully understand how the organization is doing financially no matter how large and complicated the nonprofit might be.

If the board has a treasurer, one of the main roles of that individual should be to make sure all the board members understand the financial reports. The board can also ask for shorter, easier to understand financial reports. Another helpful technique is to report the finances using key charts or diagrams. For example, all board members can easily grasp a bar chart of cash reserves each year for the previous ten years. Everyone can see immediately if the reserves are growing or declining.

Board afraid to act in a financial crisis: If a nonprofit loses a major funding source, or if it has unanticipated major expenses, a board will want to know that the organizational leader has a plan for handling the situation. If there is no plan, the board should ask for one. If the organizational leader doesn't know what to do, then the board needs to step in and act decisively to avert organizational harm.

Some board members will be reluctant to act because it violates the principles of policy-based governance. Making financial decisions involves opening the black box and making changes. But if the organizational leader does not know what to do, the board will need to become a managing board for a while until the financial crisis is averted. Managing boards may also avoid acting because they are unsure what to do. In either case, the board and the organizational leader should work together as a team to chart a course through the tough times.

ORGANIZATIONAL PERFORMANCE

This area includes making sure the organization is being effective and efficient. All nonprofits need to achieve meaningful results to justify their existence.

Board unclear regarding desired outcomes: For any governing board, the weakest area of their board policy manual is usually the ends policies or desired outcomes. Many boards find it difficult to specify the results they want to achieve. Many ministries can explain what they do but find it difficult to describe what they want to accomplish in results language.

Often, boards insert mission, vision, or core values in this section because they are unsure how to state their organizational ends. Sometimes they describe their operating philosophy. Sometimes they list important programs and services they offer. For a governing board, ends policies, or desired outcomes, should clearly cover results, recipients, and cost. Sometimes, all of these are missing.

Board unclear regarding strategy: Every board should be able to articulate the strategy their organization is using to move forward, whether they helped create it or not. But many boards feel uncertain. They may point to a strategic plan the board adopted but cannot explain the strategy undergirding it. The strategy is simply the path for how the organization is going to go from here to there.

Any board can ask the organizational leader for an updated strategy. If he or she cannot produce it, the board can get to work together with the organizational leader to create it. The strategy ought to be so straightforward and clearly explained that any board member can understand it.

Board does not monitor results: If a governing board has ambiguous or missing ends policies, it will have a difficult time monitoring organizational results. What are they supposed to measure, satisfaction level of clients? Most organizations resort to reporting on output rather than outcomes. Output is a measure of activity in the black box. For example, an organization can report that they had 752 children enrolled in their summer program, an 18% increase from the previous year. But did the children learn anything?

Results for many nonprofits will mean life change for individuals, families, or communities. Life change can be difficult to describe and measure, but meaningful life change will certainly show itself in changed behavior. These behaviors and other indicators can be identified and tracked. In general, a rough measure of a significant result is better than an accurate measure of an inconsequential result.

Organization is underperforming: A nonprofit can underperform in several ways. It can be operating inefficiently and wasting resources. It can be missing opportunities for growth and increased access to resources. It can be riding the downhill side of the organizational lifecycle. Board meetings for underperforming organizations ought to feel uncomfortable.

Managing boards, together with the organizational leader, should be looking at ways to improve operations. Governing boards should be pointing to existing results and asking how the organization can become more effective. Navigating boards should be assessing the match between the existing services and what is needed in the relevant environment. Everybody in the organization should be working together to improve overall performance.

EXECUTIVE DEVELOPMENT

This area includes all board interactions with the organizational leader to support the him or her both personally and professionally.

Board is not providing support: After a board hires an organizational leader, they will want to provide professional and emotional support to allow him or her to do the best job possible. But some boards treat the organizational leader in an impersonal way or with disrespect. Some boards are highly political with some of the board supporting and some of the board criticizing.

If a board is paying a lot of money for a competent, skilled organizational leader, they should support that person fully and work together closely with him or her. The board should ensure that the organizational leader has a professional development plan and a budget to support it. Even when disagreements happen in the board meetings, they should reach a resolution and agree to keep moving forward together.

Board struggles to provide accountability: All boards need to provide an appropriate level of accountability for the organizational leader. Sometimes boards are too timid as a group to provide that accountability. Other times, an organizational leader is powerful enough that he or she resists any efficacious accountability.

At all costs, the board needs to retain its ultimate authority over the organizational leader. It cannot let the organizational leader also run the board. It cannot let the organizational leader impede the board's fiduciary duties. By law, the board must act as responsible caretakers of the organization.

Board is neglecting succession: One of the board's primary responsibilities is ensuring leadership continuity. When the time comes for a retirement or leadership transition for another reason, the board should have in place processes for replacing the organizational leader. But too many boards don't want to ask an older leader about retirement. Too many boards assume the next organizational leader will be easy to find.

No matter how far away retirement might be, every board should ask its organizational leader for a "window" for retirement. Assuming they want to stay with the organization over the long haul, what would be the earliest date and the latest date for retirement? Younger leaders may find this to be a difficult question to answer, but a skillful board can help them determine some parameters.

Then a board needs to decide if the organization has any potential, internal candidates to replace the organizational leader. If so, they should ensure these employees have individual development plans to fill in any skill gaps that may exist. For example, an organizational leader may have no fundraising experience. A development officer may have no direct field experience. Neither may have had no formal leadership training.

Building a pipeline for succession is clearly board work.

Organizational leader is ineffectual: Sometimes, organizational leaders lose their edge. This might be because the organization has outgrown the ability of the leader. It could also be caused by problems at home or with health. If the organizational leader is no longer performing adequately for any reason, the board needs to step in.

Managing boards can offer to assist with areas where the organizational leader is underperforming. Governing boards want to stay out of operations, so if the organizational leader is not performing, they will need to reassign or terminate the individual and select a new one. Navigating boards will be less concerned about the performance of the organizational leader and more concerned about making the changes needed for the survival of the organization or for moving out to new opportunities. Most likely, the current organizational leader won't be a part of this new direction.

COMMUNICATION AND COMPLIANCE

This area includes all reporting to regulatory agencies and to donors or moral owners of an organization.

Board is unsure about mandatory reporting: Often, the board does not know what reports need to be submitted annually to the federal, state, or provincial governments, as well as other health or accreditation agencies. They tend to rely on staff to stay current with those details. But these are the kind of details that, if missed, can shut down an organization.

All boards should have a checklist of all reports that must be sent to governing bodies or accrediting agencies. These can be added to the board's annual calendar or topics for board meetings. Board members cannot afford to be willfully ignorant of what is required by the government. The legal duty of obedience specifies that boards need to make sure that the organization is fulfilling all legal requirements and obeying all applicable laws.

Board communicates poorly: The board of any nonprofit needs to identify its moral owners and communicate regularly with them and all other key stakeholders. But most boards are so consumed with their own work and the immediate challenges their organization is facing, they easily forget about others who have an interest in the organization.

Boards usually have several ways they can communicate with moral owners and stakeholders. They can issue statements directly from the board, they can issue statements through the organizational leader, and they can communicate with individuals who have questions or concerns.

Board members fail to represent the organization: Board members usually have a responsibility or expectation to serve as an ambassador for the organization, speaking positively to the larger community. For too many board members, this is an afterthought. They only think about the organization when they are in board meetings or preparing for them. Unfortunately, some board members even denigrate the work the organization is doing.

As they move through their ordinary routine in life, board members should speak positively about the organization and invite others to participate in events, volunteer their time, and give financially.

OVERALL EFFECTIVENESS

This area includes the desire for continuous improvement at all levels of the organization, good stewardship of resources, and the board evaluating its own performance.

Board intervenes too slowly or too quickly: Why can't boards do better at getting their timing right? Sometimes they wait way too long before acting and sometimes they intervene when their help is not needed or wanted. Part of the problem is that they are acting as a group, which requires more time to reach agreement. Also, board members tend to be a group of volunteers who only meet a few times a year. That is why governing boards delegate management to the organizational leader.

All boards should intervene cautiously. This is because they can easily make things worse rather than better. In general, they should only intervene in operations when a major problem has emerged or is about to hit. Managing boards that are already intervening should stick to a higher level of management. Governing boards should avoid intervening as much as possible but monitor the situation closely and support the organizational leader. Navigating boards ought to ignore the minor concerns of how the current organization is being managed and focus on what assets and programs the organization will bring with them into the future.

Board does not steward resources well: All boards should ensure that donations and assets of the organization are being well-managed. No one wants to donate money to a nonprofit that is going to waste their gift.

Boards need to monitor where donations and fees are coming from, how efficiently they are being used, and what results the resources are producing. Boards need to confirm that resources are directed toward fulfilling the mission.

Board does not improve overall productivity: Ideally, a board should make a significant contribution to the organization, either by increasing resources, increasing efficiency of operations, or increasing results. But too many boards get in the way and become a net negative for the organization. They take up staff time for preparing and reporting and sometimes hold up important decisions. Board meetings also cost money, especially if the organization is reimbursing board members for travel expenses and paying for group meals.

Managing boards are opening the black box and trying to make things better. Governing boards are over the box, watching resources coming in and results being produced, then asking how it all can be improved. Navigating boards are stepping in and making major changes to increase relevance and improve future productivity.

Board has no system for improving its own governance: Most boards tend to ignore its own issues. As a board, they are focused on working on the organization and not on themselves. But no other group can work on the board or hold it responsible for improving its own processes.

Every board needs to conduct a self-assessment at least once a year to evaluate how well it is performing. This can be done with a governance inventory or by an open and frank discussion about how the board is functioning together. It can be scheduled as part of an annual board retreat.

CHAPTER 11

BOARD BREAKTHROUGHS

Any board can get better at governance by adopting methods and procedures that improve effectiveness. Following are promising practices that have been proven by experience to improve board functioning and are suitable for wide adoption.

As a board, select the practices appropriate for immediate implementation and those the board will want to adopt in the future. It may take several years for a board to incorporate most of these promising practices. Start with what will bring the biggest benefit now.

OPTIMIZE BOARD STRUCTURE

Occasionally, a board will want to take a fresh look at how it operates and make some adjustments. The board can decide to right-size if they are too large for efficient functioning, or too small for an adequate range of perspectives. It can determine the ideal size range, number of meetings per year, and rethink length of terms and term limits. For example, a board may make the decision to transition from a managing board to a governing board. For some organizations, this will require a bylaw change and an approval from organizational members. Other boards can simply adjust their current bylaws and move to a more optimum structure.

USE COMMITTEES SPARINGLY

Some boards have standing committees that meet at the same time as the full board or in between meetings. Sometimes the organization must make up work for the committees to do. When the committees report to the full board, sometimes their recommendations are overturned, or the discussion and decision is remade with the full board. If there is board work to be assigned, it is better to use ad hoc committees or temporary task force groups. When their assignment is accomplished, they no longer meet. Some boards retain their committee structure but simply stop meeting as committees and keep the entire board together for the full meeting.

MAKE THE ORGANIZATIONAL LEADER EX OFFICIO

With an increasing demand for accountability of nonprofits and their organizational leaders, it makes sense to make the organizational leader a member of the board *ex officio*, which means "from the office." The organizational leader is automatically in the board meetings without having to be elected or approved by a vote.

The organizational leader can serve with or without a formal power to vote. People tend to feel strongly about this one way or the other. Some say the organizational leader should have a vote to help him or her feel legitimate and a true part of the board. Others feel the organizational leader should serve without vote to make clear he or she reports to the board. In practice, it does not matter whether the organizational leader has a vote if the board is striving for consensus anyway.

Some nonprofits have the organizational leader also serve as the board chair. In our post-Enron culture, most businesses are moving away from that practice. Similarly, more nonprofits are also separating the roles of organizational leader and board chair to increase the chances for a stronger level of accountability.

BUILD A RECRUITMENT PIPELINE

All too often, recruitment of new board members is handled casually. During a board meeting, the board chair asks for names of someone who would be a good fit for an open position. Then the organizational leader or a couple board members meet with the individual and ask him or her to serve. But the new board member may be unknown to the rest of the board and has usually not been properly vetted.

Nonprofits can avoid this by building a pipeline for new board members. For example, they can hold special donor gatherings and get to know people who are already genuinely committed to the organization. They can work side-by-side with volunteers or hold special appreciation events to get to know them. Boards can also create special task forces or committees, such as a fundraising committee or special event team, to observe which people have the best potential to serve on the board. Then they can compare these individuals with their list of desired capabilities or perspectives to make an informed decision.

ASSEMBLE AN ORIENTATION KIT

Most new board members receive a skimpy orientation. They may feel unsure about their role and basically watch and learn during the first several meetings. Boards that do not provide any orientation assume that new board members will soon get the hang of it. It would be better if they were prepared to start contributing from their first meeting.

An orientation kit should include the organizational handbook or board policy manual, minutes from the past year or so, current promotional material, a short history of the organization, a job description and expectations, an organization chart, short bios of the other board members, a strategic plan or annual plan, and a book or a few articles explaining the governance type of this board.

The organization should also have a clear orientation process that specifies who meets with the new board member, whether there is a tour of the office or facility, and when the new board member will have an appointment with the organizational leader.

ESTABLISH JOB DESCRIPTIONS

Even if the main responsibilities of board members are listed in the bylaws, all board members will benefit from having a more detailed job description as a separate document or built into the governing policies. Besides the officers, at-large board members should have a written job description as well.

Good job descriptions include position title, a brief description of the role, main responsibilities, and a statement about what expenses are reimbursable.

CLARIFY EXPECTATIONS

Along with the job description, any other expectations should be written in a code of conduct document or included in the board policy manual. Expectations can spell out inappropriate behavior to be avoided in board meetings, keeping information and opinions confidential, who to notify if not able to attend a board meeting, attendance at special events, and their role in fundraising.

Rightful use of authority should also be made clear. Bob Andringa has written about the four hats board members may wear. The *governance hat* is worn when the board formally gathers for a meeting and a quorum is present. The authority of the board is held by the board as a group, not by individual board members. When the board meeting is over, the governance hat stays in the board room. The *implementor hat* is worn when one or more individuals is given work to do for the board. The authority for them to act is specifically given to them by the board. For example, a board member may be asked to negotiate a price for purchasing land or a building. When the task is complete the authority returns to the board as a group. The *participant hat* is worn when board members are asked to attend a special event. In this case, they are officially representing the board. The *volunteer hat* is worn any other time board members encounter the organization. They have no governing authority or responsibility apart from the board as a group. When they serve as a volunteer in the work, they report to a staff person and work under their authority.

GENERATE AN ANNUAL CALENDAR

As a part of the board policy manual, the board should have a calendar of topics to be addressed or work to be done each time they meet. For example, a board may want to ask for a budget narrative in September, a draft budget in October, and a final budget in November. A bylaw review can be scheduled for every June. A governing board will want to review a certain section of their board policy manual throughout the year.

This is useful for the board chair when combined with a typical agenda. The board chair takes the typical agenda and adds the appropriate items from the annual calendar, plus any other discussion items that have emerged. These tools keep the board on schedule and prevent the board from neglecting important agenda items when they meet.

ESTABLISH A MONITORING SCHEDULE

To avoid micromanaging, a managing board or a governing board can set up a schedule for routine monitoring. These monitoring reports can be spread out through the year. For example, the board may have a policy that the organization be adequately insured. They may ask to see evidence of this every summer. The organizational leader can inspect all the insurances, adjust coverage as needed, and write a monitoring report detailing all insurances, amounts, and due dates for renewal. With a monitoring schedule, the board avoids micromanaging and the organizational leader is not surprised by a sudden request for proof of compliance to a limitations policy.

EMAIL REPORTS AND HANDOUTS

For board members to adequately prepare for meetings, all reports, handouts, and background reading should be mailed or emailed ahead of time. A governing board can specify how many days in advance in their board policy manual. The board members can then print the reports on their own or bring their electronic device to the meeting to access the documents. Some board members prefer to work with paper, and some prefer electronic access.

When an organizational leader distributes handouts in a meeting, or worse, compiles a binder filled with documents, board members will tend to become distracted and read the materials instead of listening to the organizational leader or participating in the discussion.

ARRANGE THE MEETING SPACE

Pay attention to the room layout to allow for comfortable and healthy communication. A long, rectangular table does not allow for everyone to see each other. Someone sitting in the middle must lean forward and look both ways to address the group. If tables and chairs are moveable, a room layout with the tables in a circle, square, or horseshoe arrangement allows for better discussion. If audio-visual equipment will be used, make sure everyone will be able to comfortably view the presentation.

SERVE REFRESHMENTS AND TAKE BREAKS

Often, board meetings run nonstop because there is too much material to cover in too little time. But taking breaks and offering refreshments can boost board effectiveness. Most adults appreciate a "bio break" every 90-120 minutes. Ignore this practice and people will be going in and out of the meeting at various intervals, sometimes disrupting discussion. For shorter board meetings, even offering coffee, tea, or water makes a positive difference for board members. Healthy snacks can provide a needed boost of energy during an early morning or evening meeting.

SCHEDULE EXECUTIVE SESSIONS

An executive session during a board meeting is a closed discussion of just the board members. Some recommend this at the beginning of each board meeting, some at the end, and some at both beginning and end. Adding a regular executive session to every board meeting allows the board to speak freely without the organizational leader present and prevents the organizational leader from getting nervous. If a board does not make this a regular practice, then asks the organizational leader to be excused for an executive session, the leader may worry needlessly. Also, this reduces the need board members feel for a "meeting before the meeting" or a "parking lot meeting" afterwards. A board should hold an executive session every time they meet, whether they feel the need for it or not.

USE A CONSENT AGENDA

A consent agenda is a technique for officially receiving reports and approving routine reports that do not need to be discussed individually. The board chair will group these reports together and ask if any board member wishes to discuss any of them. After those reports are removed, the board votes to receive or approve the rest. Then the ones removed can be discussed as a board. Using the consent agenda technique can save a significant amount of time for boards.

CREATE A DASHBOARD

In business, a dashboard is a visual display of data with all the key indicators in one report. Nonprofit organizations can also create a dashboard of key indicators for their organization. The data can be displayed as bar charts, pie diagrams, or line charts. Some may also want to color code key indicators green, yellow, and red to show if they are on target. For example, a nonprofit can show a chart of income by month for the trailing twelve months. It can show income from a special event for a trailing five years. A visual display of data is more appealing to most board members than straining to read columns of numbers.

CONDUCT SURVEYS

A board can conduct a survey of any group in an organization without violating policy-based governance. The surveys can be done by telephone, using the Internet, or in person. This allows a board to keep a finger on the pulse of the organization. They can survey donors, staff, parents of children enrolled in a program, or other stakeholders. If they are only gathering information about the health of the organization, surveys are fine. Where boards get in trouble is taking that information and using it to micromanage the organizational leader or ordering program adjustments.

USE HAND SIGNALS

Managing boards need to discipline themselves to avoid micromanaging the organization. Governing boards need to avoid managing as well as micromanaging. Some boards use red cards to pause discussion if the board is getting off track. If a board member holds up a red card, the entire board can decide if they are doing board work or staff work, then get themselves back on track.

Some boards use a stop sign attached to a small stick to do the same. A simple hand signal will also work, such as "throwing a T" for a brief timeout. This is an invaluable practice for boards transitioning from managing to governing. It is also useful for corralling new board members who are hooked on micromanaging.

STRIVE FOR CONSENSUS

As much as possible, most boards should strive to achieve consensus for all their decisions and official actions. But some misunderstand the meaning of consensus. It does not mean that everybody fully agrees. It means that while all are not in full agreement, the minority understands the reasoning behind the decision and can agree to support it outside the board meeting. This also makes it easier for the board to maintain confidentiality and to speak with one voice.

Striving for complete agreement can slow a board down to a crawl. Sometimes, complete agreement is just not possible. As a last resort, or when time is too short, the board chair should call for a simple vote to determine the matter and move on.

EVALUATE EVERY MEETING

Most boards can afford the time to do a short feedback session at the close of every meeting. A few self-assessment questions as a part of the typical agenda can be useful. They can simply ask what went well and what needs improvement. Or they can ask more specific questions like:

- Did we treat each other with respect?
- Did we listen to each other carefully and avoid overtalking?
- Did we work together as a team?
- Did we focus on the organization's needs and not our own?
- Did we stick to governing and stay out of managing?
- Did we stay out of the weeds?
- Does anyone want to offer an apology for anything?

CONDUCT AN ANNUAL PERFORMANCE REVIEW

The organizational leader deserves to know how he or she is doing. Normal board feedback can feel ambiguous. But the process differs according to type of board.

Managing boards will conduct a performance appraisal like how it is done in well-managed businesses. The full board, or one of the board members, will meet with the organizational leader to establish expectations and performance standards or goals. The board will provide feedback along the way during the rest of the year. At the appointed time, the board will measure actual performance and compare this with the standards or goals. If done well, the board will ask the organizational leader to self-assess and then discuss where they agree or disagree. Together, they will come up with corrective measures and plans for moving forward. The goal is professional growth and performance improvement.

Governing boards have delegated management and do not want to supervise the organizational leader. Instead, they want to provide encouragement and accountability. Accordingly, governing boards do not focus on individual performance of the organizational leader, but on the performance of the organization. Specifically, they will want to know what progress has been made on organizational ends over the past year and what limitations policies have been exceeded. If annual goals were set together the year before, the board may review those as a part of the progress toward achieving organizational results. Some may also want to ensure that the organizational leader has a plan for professional development. They should not decide the plan or approve it. They should simply make sure a plan is in place and funding for it is in the budget.

IMPLEMENT A SUCCESSION PLANNING PROCESS

Succession planning is routinely ignored by boards of small and large organizations. Often, board members don't want to offend the organizational leader by asking about retirement plans. Some abdicate their duty by letting the current leader pick the next one. Boards need two kinds of succession plans. An emergency succession plan details who would step in as acting organizational leader in the even the current leader was suddenly incapacitated for several months. A general succession plan identifies potential successors of the organizational leader and describes leadership development plans for these individuals. For larger organizations, the succession plan may be extended to cover a few other key staff positions, for example, director of development. The point of having a succession plan and reviewing it annually is to provide leadership continuity for the organization.

TAKE TIME TO BUILD RELATIONSHIPS

Many of the problems that boards face are basically people problems. If a board does not take time to build relationships, foster teamwork, and establish trust, it will be more difficult for the group to work together productively. This is magnified with term limits and new board members continually joining the group.

An effective board will take time to build quality relationships between board members. Any board can take some time in a board meeting for personal sharing. For boards that require travel, the first evening can be dedicated to informal conversation with a purpose. Meals can be organized to break down barriers and allow people to get to know each other in a relaxed atmosphere. Boards that meet one evening per month can start an hour earlier with a shared meal.

Boards that do not take time to build relationships will tend to spend the time they saved solving problems and resolving unnecessary conflicts. This is so basic, but many boards miss it because they feel pressed for time during their meetings.

ENGAGE BOARD MEMBERS IN FIELD OBSERVATION

In order to properly oversee an organization, board members need to have a rudimentary understanding of the work it does. With some nonprofits, like a local church, board members have an opportunity to observe every week. With others, such as an international organization, it is costly to fly the entire board to see the work. Some nonprofits require board members to also serve in a volunteer role in the organization. But boards tend to neglect this because they don't want to ask board members to take more time out of their already busy lives. Technology makes this practice easier than ever. Plus, personally observing what is happening may inspire board members to contribute more time, money, and energy to the organization.

SCHEDULE BOARD RETREATS

An annual retreat is recommended for most boards. The retreat does not have to be off-site. It does not need to be overnight if all the participants are local. A full-day or multi-day retreat allows for building relationships and adequate time to think strategically together. Even small nonprofits might be able to secure a meeting room at a business at no cost for an all-day Saturday meeting.

Staying at a resort or retreat center can also serve as a thank you to board members who are generously donating their time and expertise. Managing boards can do their annual planning together with the organizational leader on a retreat. Governing boards can refine ends policies on a retreat. Navigating boards will have the time to explore new options together.

COMPLETE A BOARD SELF-ASSESSMENT

Every couple of years, a board would be wise to complete a comprehensive self-assessment (like the one in the appendix). These online or paper and pencil inventories allow boards to quickly identify their highest and lowest scoring areas. This will allow them to build on strengths and take corrective action regarding areas needing improvement.

HIGHLIGHT BOARD MEMBERS

Some nonprofit boards mistakenly think they should keep their board members out of public scrutiny. But for many nonprofits, making known who is on your board can be a simple way to build trust. Major donors will be more willing to give if they have confidence in the board. Besides listing names on a website, more trust can be gained by sharing photos and human-interest details. For example, how did they get connected to the organization? What are they passionate about in life? What do they do for a living?

Members and clients might not be especially interested in who serves on the board or what the board does, but openness about the board can help build trust. Any organization can dedicate a page on their website with information about the board members. Organizations with buildings and regular gatherings can dedicate a wall to photos and information about current board members.

SECURE OUTSIDE COACHING

Nonprofit board members tend to think they have to figure out governance on their own. But any board can get paid or volunteer coaching from others with extensive experience. For example, a new board chair who would like some coaching on leading the board can find a former board chair or a professional coach. An organizational leader and a board chair not on the same page can find help to learn how to work together without getting in each other's way. A board that wants to make a major transition can find someone who has led it before. Navigating boards especially should look for outside people who can lend them the expertise they need to forge a new strategic direction for their organization.

COMMIT TO ONGOING LEARNING

All boards should set aside time in their schedule and a line item in their budget for ongoing board education. One approach is to set a goal of reading one book a year together as a board. The book can be about governance or about the field in which they are serving. Another approach is to invite a community leader or nonprofit leader to a meeting to update the board regarding changes in the relevant environment. Some boards are reluctant to buy books or hire a resource person for fear of being accused of spending money on themselves. Some boards resist because they feel too busy. But a small investment in board education can enhance the ability of the board to make a significant contribution to the organization. Isn't that what boards are supposed to do?

CHAPTER 12

EFFECTIVE BOARDS

Now that you have finished reading this book, you are probably eager to begin implementing some of these principles and practices. You want to do what you can to help your board become more effective.

This book is a guide for adaptive governance. Adaptive governance means that while overseeing an organization, the board keeps an eye on what is changing in the relevant environment. It looks for potential risks and ways to mitigate those risks. It regularly looks for new opportunities that may be emerging. It knows where the organization is at in terms of organizational lifecycle and makes adjustments in the way it governs as needed. Adaptive boards tend to make important contributions to the organizations they oversee.

If you sense that your board needs to transition from one type of governance to another, start by opening a deep discussion about managing, governing, and navigating boards. Make sure everyone understands how these differ. Making a transition from one type to another should be made intentionally and together. Work towards gaining a consensus, then select a specific date to make the change. Be prepared for opposition. Moving between these types should not happen just for a meeting or two. The transition to a new type should usually last several years, or until conditions change enough to justify another transition.

If your board is operating in the right mode but it wants to become more effective, the board should take on a mindset of continuous improvement. You can begin by inviting the board members to complete a self-assessment, either the one at the back of this book or any other available online. You can also recommend scheduling a board retreat to address, as a group, how the board can function more effectively. Keep in mind that ineffective boards are usually reluctant to address their own dysfunction.

You will want to incorporate many of the best practices described in this book. Start with smaller and easier changes. As they experience immediate benefits, the board's openness to change will increase. Remember that old habits die hard. But many small changes can significantly increase board effectiveness over time.

Boards ought to be mindful regarding their own performance. But most are not. When they meet, the agenda is full, and time is short. They feel pressure to focus on the current organizational issues. Who has time to worry about whether the board is being effective?

Effective boards are not afraid to address the biggest issues and challenges the organization is facing. If the organization is in decline, the board should talk about it. If the world is changing and the organization needs to adapt, the board should open a discussion about what needs to change. You may need to be the person to bring up the issue that nobody wants to talk about. You may need to be the one who states the obvious.

Rebekah Basinger, a governance coach, wrote her doctoral dissertation on boards. During her research, she carefully studied the minutes of four small colleges going back 25 years. One of her findings was that these boards certainly talked about the problems their institutions were facing, but they never seemed to get around to addressing them.

Warning: plot twist ahead. Implementation of these principles and practices is seldom straightforward. You cannot simply pick a problem, solve it, and move on to the next one. The problems boards encounter are usually difficult to resolve because of their level of complexity.

COMPLEX PROBLEMS

Effective boards work on their problems. They address challenges their organization is facing as well as any dysfunctional behavior of their own as a group. But this requires courage.

Problems are not created equal. Boards that want to be effective realize there are different kinds of problems requiring different solution approaches. Organizational leaders and their boards face tame, messy, and wicked problems.

A design theorist, Horst Rittel, coined the term "wicked" for problems that are ill-defined and complex. There may be several ways to frame the problem. Sometimes, the problem is not understood until a solution is found. Requirements may be changing while time is running out. For these problems, there is no single solution or right answer. They are technically complex.

A pioneer in the systems thinking movement, Russ Ackoff, coined the term "mess" for a set of interrelated problems that resist solution. These may include interpersonal conflicts, lack of data, economic constraints, and numerous intervention points. Rather than being solved, messes are usually managed at best. Because they involve social systems, these problems are socially complex.

Combining technical complexity with social complexity results in four kinds of problems that boards will encounter. Dealing effectively with technical complexity requires board members who have cognitive skills. Dealing effectively with social complexity requires board members who have relational skills.

	LOW SOCIAL COMPLEXITY	HIGH SOCIAL COMPLEXITY
HIGH TECHNICAL COMPLEXITY	Wicked Problems	Wicked Messes
LOW TECHNICAL COMPLEXITY	Tame Problems	Messy Problems

Tame problems can be resolved using a straightforward approach to find an acceptable solution. They are not always easy problems to solve, but at least the board has a standard process to follow. 1) Define the problem. 2) Gather information. 3) Brainstorm possible solutions. 4) Weigh the pros and cons of each. 5) Make a decision. 6) Implement the solution. Tame problems have fewer gray areas. Every board member understands the problem, sees what needs to happen, and agrees on the best way forward.

Wicked problems do not offer a straightforward approach to finding a solution. They are problems with unclear edges and are often difficult to define. They can be viewed from several perspectives. Board members have difficulty grasping the problem and generating workable solutions. They may involve competing values or require specialized knowledge. A board cannot approach these like tame problems. They will need to use advanced analytical methods and possibly bring in experts for assistance. Several possible solutions may be identified, but none of them fully acceptable. Boards struggle to achieve consensus with these kinds of problems.

Messy problems involve interactions within and between social systems. For example, two board members don't get along with each other. Staff and board see each other as "us versus them." A staff member is related to a board member. Somebody is passed over for a promotion. People liked things the way they were. Boards cannot approach these like wicked problems. More information and more analysis may not help. Messy problems require board members who have emotional intelligence and people skills. It requires an awareness of group dynamics. Messy problems dealt with poorly can lead to an erosion of trust in the board.

Wicked messes are a combination of both complexities. These problems may take a long time to resolve or even be intractable. Sometimes, they involve several problems with interrelated factors. Wicked messes have the potential to split an organization, anger staff, or disappoint clients. Every attempted solution tends to cause another problem. Boards may decide to try to clean up the mess, let it dissipate naturally, or declare it a new normal.

Effective boards need both IQ and EQ, both cognitive intelligence and emotional intelligence, to deal with the complex problems they encounter. Don't become discouraged if you experience resistance when you try to help the board, or your organization become more effective.

NEXT STEPS

Effective boards work on their problems. What are your next steps?

It does not matter whether you are the board chair, a board member, or the organizational leader. Anyone can suggest that the board spend some time reflecting on the type of board it ought to be. Anyone can suggest that the board work to improve its level of effectiveness. Anyone can urge the board to pay more attention to the organization's relative environment. Anyone can suggest that the board consider adopting specific, new practices.

Do what you can to maximize board effectiveness. Start now.

APPENDIX

Discussion Guide
Board Self-Assessment
About the Author
Additional Resources

DISCUSSION GUIDE

Use the following questions to stimulate conversation about increasing the effectiveness of your board. After giving each board member a copy of the book, you can work through it one chapter per meeting, three chapters per meeting, or simply pick and choose the chapters that are most relevant to your situation right now.

1. WHY BOARDS UNDERPERFORM

- What insights did you glean from the minimart story?

- How much does it cost your organization in meals, travel expenses, and staff time to make arrangements for all board meetings for one year?

- What does your board provide in an attempt to make a net contribution to the organization?

2. GOVERNANCE CONFUSION

- What were you confused about when you first joined this board?

- Which pair of items in the list would you like to discuss further?

- What other boards have you served on and what did you learn from those experiences?

3. THREE TYPES OF BOARDS

- How should your board members fulfil their legal duty of care on this board?

- What new insights did you get from the black box metaphor?

- Which type of board is yours and which do you want it to be?

4. MANAGING BOARDS

- When have you observed an effective managing board in action?

- What temptations do members of managing boards face?

- In your opinion, what is the most important factor for success as a managing board?

5. GOVERNING BOARDS

- When have you observed an effective governing board in action?

- What temptations do members of governing boards face?

- In your opinion, what is the most important factor for success as a governing board?

6. NAVIGATING BOARDS

- When have you observed an effective navigating board in action?

- What temptations do members of navigating boards face?

- In your opinion, what is the most important factor for success as a navigating board?

7. MAKING A TRANSITION

- When have you experienced any of these transitions in the past?

- Which of these transitions do you believe your board needs to make now?

- What obstacles do you expect that your board and organization will encounter?

8. THE BOARD'S ROLE IN STRATEGY

- What level of involvement do you believe your board should have in strategy formation?

- Where are you at on the organizational lifecycle and what type of strategy do you currently have?

- What would be the right rhythm for your board to conduct seasonal strategic reviews?

9. THE BOARD'S ROLE IN FUNDRAISING

- When you were invited to serve on this board, to what degree were expectations regarding personal giving and fundraising communicated to you?

- What is the board's current role in fundraising and what would you like it to be?

- What is your organization's current mix of fundraising tactics and what new opportunities do you see?

10. BOARD BREAKDOWNS

- Which of these board breakdowns is your organization experiencing?

- What underlying factors are allowing these breakdowns to continue?

- Which should be the first breakdowns the board should address and how should you do this?

11. BOARD BREAKTHROUGHS

- How many of these governance best practices are you currently implementing?

- What are the top five you would like to see your board adopt?

- What prevents your board from spending time on becoming more effective?

12. EFFECTIVE BOARDS

- What does adaptive governance mean for this board?

- What are some examples of wicked problems your organization deals with?

- What are some examples of messy problems your organization deals with?

BOARD SELF-ASSESSMENT

On an annual basis, a board should assess its structure, composition, and overall effectiveness. Following are questions that a board can use for a self-assessment. Have each board member complete the assessment and then discuss reasons for low scores and suggestions for improvement.

Mark your answer using the following scale:
5 = We are excelling in this area
4 = We are doing well, no change needed
3 = We need to discuss improvements
2 = We need to make some minor adjustments
1 = We need to make significant changes

BOARD STRUCTURE	
1. We have the optimal number of board members on our board	5 4 3 2 1
2. We have the right number of meetings per year to do our work	5 4 3 2 1
3. We have a good process for recruiting new board members	5 4 3 2 1
4. We have a thorough process for orienting new board members	5 4 3 2 1
5. We have selected a clear governing style	5 4 3 2 1
6. The roles of the organizational leader and the board chair are clear to all	5 4 3 2 1
7. The organizational leader is an ex officio board member but without vote	5 4 3 2 1
8. The organizational leader is responsible for recruiting, hiring, evaluating, and terminating all other staff	5 4 3 2 1
9. The board chair and organizational leader communicate regularly to coordinate efforts	5 4 3 2 1

BOARD MEMBERS	
10. Our board members are passionate about our mission and vision	5 4 3 2 1
11. Our board members are knowledgeable about the organization and its programs	5 4 3 2 1
12. Our board members understand best practices of governance	5 4 3 2 1
13. Our board has a defined profile of the desirable characteristics and mix of skills we are looking for in new board members	5 4 3 2 1
14. We build a list of potential board candidates through the year	5 4 3 2 1
15. Our board as a whole contains all the knowledge and skills we need on the board	5 4 3 2 1
16. Our board members are loyal to the organization and committed to our cause	5 4 3 2 1
17. We have a written job description for the board chair	5 4 3 2 1
18. We have a written job description for all other officers	5 4 3 2 1
19. We have a written job description for regular board members	5 4 3 2 1
20. We have a written code of conduct that all board members adhere to	5 4 3 2 1
21. We have a conflict of interest statement that board members sign each year	5 4 3 2 1
22. The board makes it a practice to honor board members when they depart	5 4 3 2 1
BOARD MEETINGS	
23. We have a standard format for setting our agenda that functions well	5 4 3 2 1
24. Board meetings are neither too long nor too short	5 4 3 2 1
25. The board chair facilitates the board meetings adequately	5 4 3 2 1
26. The board uses a consent agenda to maximize time on strategic issues	5 4 3 2 1
27. Board members are engaged in discussion and dialogue with each other	5 4 3 2 1

28. Board members listen deeply and show respect for each other	5 4 3 2 1
29. Handouts are kept to the minimum we need to do our work	5 4 3 2 1
30. The board uses short-term, ad hoc committees for specialized issues	5 4 3 2 1
31. We have access to the information we need to monitor organizational performance	5 4 3 2 1
32. The reports are board-driven not staff-driven	5 4 3 2 1
33. The board specifies the reports it wants	5 4 3 2 1
34. Every board meeting includes a short executive session at the beginning or end of each meeting	5 4 3 2 1
35. Board meetings include time for board education and social interaction	5 4 3 2 1
36. The board schedules regular retreats to build relationships and focus on strategy	5 4 3 2 1
37. The board assesses its behavior at the end of every meeting and makes suggestions for improvement	5 4 3 2 1
BOARD POLICIES	
38. The board has written policies in one place that are easily accessible	5 4 3 2 1
39. The board policies are brief yet comprehensive	5 4 3 2 1
40. One section of our board policy manual describes desired outcomes	5 4 3 2 1
41. One section of our board policy manual describes staff limitations	5 4 3 2 1
42. One section of our board policy manual describes board and staff relationship and roles	5 4 3 2 1
43. One section of our board policy manual describes how our board does its work	5 4 3 2 1
44. The board policies mean what they say, and board members agree with them	5 4 3 2 1
45. The board policies are up-to-date and reviewed at least annually	5 4 3 2 1
46. The board actively governs using written policies	5 4 3 2 1

FIDUCIARY RESPONSIBILITY

47. Our board members are generous donors who are financially invested in the organization	5 4 3 2 1
48. Board members understand their role in fundraising activities and fulfill it	5 4 3 2 1
49. Board members network effectively to raise funds and extend the reach of the organization	5 4 3 2 1
50. The board has an income strategy to ensure adequate resources for the organization	5 4 3 2 1
51. Board members understand the budget and financial reports	5 4 3 2 1
52. The board actively monitors actual financial condition and projections	5 4 3 2 1
53. The board is willing to take action to correct a financial shortfall	5 4 3 2 1

ORGANIZATIONAL PERFORMANCE

54. The board has measures of organizational results and focuses on them	5 4 3 2 1
55. The board determines or approves strategic direction for the organization	5 4 3 2 1
56. The board monitors strategic initiatives	5 4 3 2 1
57. The board encourages a culture of transparency, integrity, and accountability at all levels	5 4 3 2 1
58. The board effectively oversees overall organizational performance	5 4 3 2 1

EXECUTIVE DEVELOPMENT

59. The board delegates responsibility through the organizational leader	5 4 3 2 1
60. The board holds the organizational leader accountable for results	5 4 3 2 1
61. The board does not micromanage or interfere with organizational leader performance	5 4 3 2 1
62. The board evaluates organizational leader performance on an annual basis	5 4 3 2 1

63. The board oversees succession planning	5 4 3 2 1
64. The board determines the compensation package for the organizational leader	5 4 3 2 1
65. The board actively supports and encourages the organizational leader	5 4 3 2 1
COMMUNICATION AND COMPLIANCE	
66. The board makes sure the organization has adequate insurance	5 4 3 2 1
67. The board makes sure the organization meets all legal requirements	5 4 3 2 1
68. The board keeps the moral owners of the organization adequately informed	5 4 3 2 1
69. The board guards well the integrity of the organization	5 4 3 2 1
70. Board members act as ambassadors of the organization to our constituency and the wider community	5 4 3 2 1
OVERALL EFFECTIVENESS	
71. Board members understand that they are trustees for the moral owners and carry out their duties faithfully	5 4 3 2 1
72. The board effectively stewards the resources of the organization	5 4 3 2 1
73. The board effectively improves the overall productivity of the organization	5 4 3 2 1
74. The board effectively helps the organization achieve sustainable mission fulfillment	5 4 3 2 1
75. The board has a system to monitor key indicators of organizational performance	5 4 3 2 1
76. Then board knows why, when, and how it would close or merge with another organization if needed	5 4 3 2 1
77. The board has a system for continuously improving its governance process	5 4 3 2 1

This assessment is available from the author as an online survey with a report of the compiled results and live feedback. Contact jim@galvinandassociates.com.

ABOUT THE AUTHOR

James C. Galvin is an organizational consultant specializing in strategy, governance, and change. He is relentlessly focused on releasing the potential of leaders and organizations.

His client list spans a wide variety of organizations including foundations, associations, universities, agencies, ministries, congregations, denominations, and businesses.

Jim holds the Doctor of Education degree in Curriculum and Supervision from Northern Illinois University, where the faculty nominated his doctoral research for the prestigious Dissertation of the Year Award. He holds the Masters degree in Christian Formation and Ministry from Wheaton College where he also completed his undergraduate work in Christian Education.

Jim has served as Adjunct Faculty at Wheaton College and Judson University for over a decade. In addition, he serves as the managing partner for the Alliance for Board Effectiveness, a network of leading nonprofit governance consultants.

He has drawn upon his extensive experience to write many best-selling books and instructional resources published by Zondervan, Tyndale House, Thomas Nelson, Baker, Navpress, Moody, Intervarsity Press, Concordia, and Focus on the Family. He is the co-creator and co-senior editor of the *Life Application Study Bible*, one of the all-time best-selling Bible products on the market. He won the C.S. Lewis Medal Award for Children's Literature three times and has been honored by the Evangelical Christian Publisher's Association as a finalist for the Christian Book Award 19 times. Jim's products have been translated into more than 37 languages around the world.

Jim lives in Elgin, Illinois, with his wife, Kathleen. They have two adult children.

ADDITIONAL RESOURCES

Email the author: jim@galvinandassociates.com
Visit his website: www.galvinandassociates.com

BOOK SALES

For more purchasing options and information on the book, visit the publisher at www.tenthpowerpublishing.com. For quantity discounts when purchasing copies for your board, email the author directly.

CONSULTING

You are welcome to visit www.galvinandassociates.com for complimentary articles and white papers on governance and other leadership issues. Contact the author if you are interested in an online version of the Board Self-Assessment that includes a one-hour conversation with him and feedback on the results.

He also provides governance training and board consulting either in-person or by videoconference. In addition, he can facilitate your next strategic retreat. This generative planning time can be composed of board members only, staff members only, or a special task force of board, staff, and key outsiders. Email the author directly to discuss your needs.